The Divine Presence of Jesus

Meditation and Commentary on the Gospel of John

The Divine Presence of Jesus

Meditation and Commentary on the Gospel of John

Alfred McBride, O. Praem.

Our Sunday Visitor Publishing Division
Our Sunday Visitor, Inc.
Huntington, Indiana 46750

Nihil Obstat: Reverend Richard J. Murphy, O.M.I.
                 Censor Deputatus

Imprimatur: Reverend Msgr. William J. Kane, V.G.
                 Vicar General for the Archdiocese of Washington
                 October 28, 1991

The nihil obstat and imprimatur are official declarations that a book
or pamphlet is free of doctrinal or moral error. No implication is contained therein that those who have granted the nihil obstat and the imprimatur agree with the content, opinions or statements expressed.

ISBN: 0-87973-357-8
LCCCN: 91-62163

PRINTED IN THE UNITED STATES OF AMERICA

Cover design by Rebecca J. Heaston
Editorial production by Kelley L. Renz
357

Dedicated to my beloved community of St. Norbert Abbey. They have nourished me in faith and affection and to them I owe boundless gratitude. I must especially mention Abbot Sylvester Killeen, O. Praem., who has embodied so well the ideals of a gentleman and a holy man. I also express my deep admiration for Abbot Benjamin Mackin, O.Praem., whose strong religious faith has been a light for all our membership.

In addition, I include in this dedication some lifelong friends: Bob and Patricia Rupp, Jim and Dorothy Youniss, Bob and Ria Moccia, Jim and Shirley Tobias, Janet, Karl and Heather Sooder, Rose Bogan, Mary Lou Ziga, Joe and Eleanor Lopez, Lloyd and Gena McKee, Arturo and Eloisa Ortega, Bob and Ursula Lulley, John and Annette Truman, Sue Ades, Sister Kathleen Marie Shields, Sister Ann Patricia O'Connor, Mother Therese of the Spirit of Love, Sister Mary Gorman and Sister Bartholomew Marie.

Lastly, I must acknowledge the superb professional and personal service rendered to me by my editor, Kelley Renz, the generous confidence in this project shown by Robert Lockwood, Publisher at Our Sunday Visitor, and the encouragement to embark on the series by Jackie Eckert, Acquisitions Editor at Our Sunday Visitor.

As I looked, a stormwind came from the North, a huge cloud with flashing fire [enveloped in brightness], from the midst of which [the midst of the fire] something gleamed like electrum. Within it were figures resembling four living creatures that looked like this: their form was human, but each had four faces and four wings, and their legs went straight down; the soles of their feet were round. They sparkled with a gleam like burnished bronze.

Their faces were like this: each of the four had the face of a man, but on the right side was the face of a lion, and on the left side the face of an ox, and finally each had the face of an eagle. . . .

—Ezekiel 1:4-8

The four living creatures seen by Ezekiel in the vision described above are believed to symbolize the four authors of the gospels. St. John is symbolized by the eagle because the heights to which an eagle can soar are a fitting image of God's love for us.

Contents

Foreword

On the road to Emmaus, Jesus gave his two friends a Scripture lesson. He took the Bible as though it were a loaf of bread and broke it open to feed their hearts, minds, feelings, and souls. He explained how the prophets, wisdom speakers, psalm singers, storytellers, and patriarchs sang and spoke of the essential link between the sufferings of the Messiah and his glory. "Was it not necessary that the Messiah should suffer these things and so enter his glory?" (Lk. 24:6).

Luke does not give us the details of that remarkable Scripture lesson, other than to say the listeners were so moved that their hearts burned within them. Jesus gave them an experience of Scripture that caused a personal spiritual and moral conversion. The Christian interpretation of Scripture ever since has drawn two essential guidelines from that scene. First, all of Scripture illumines the meaning and purpose of Jesus Christ's work of salvation. Second, the biblical words call each of us to a faith conversion to Jesus Christ.

No interpreter of Scripture ever understood these principles better than St. Augustine. For him the soul was the home of all the feelings in the body. Since Christians were members of Christ's Body, they could get in touch with the inner life of Jesus, his soul if you will. As Augustine scanned the pages of Scripture, he found in the psalms the record of the feelings of Jesus. The psalms and the gospels were more than two books written in different periods of history, they were the seamless garment of the love story between God and people, one text illuminating the other.

The Christ of Augustine's sermons on the gospels possesses the quiet majesty of classic art. But in his commentaries on the psalms, Augustine comes upon a flood of emotions and applies them to Jesus. The figure of the passionate King David supplies the vision of the emotions of Jesus. Hence it is Christ's voice that is heard in the psalms, "a voice singing happily, a voice rejoicing in hope, a voice sighing in its present state. We should know his voice, feel it intimately, make it our own" (*Commentary on Psalms*, 42,1).

At the same time, Augustine wanted to do more than stir up feeling in the listeners to his Scripture sermons. He wanted to break bread and feed the multitude. As a boy, he had stolen fruit to share with his comrades. As a bishop, he raided the fields of Scripture to feed his parishioners to whom he ministered for forty years. "I go to feed so I can give you to eat. I lay before you that from which I draw my life" (*Fragments*, 2, 4). He was interested in converting his listeners to Jesus ever more deeply through the Scriptures.

He wrote to Jerome that he could never be a disinterested Bible scholar. "If I gain any new knowledge of Scripture, I pay it out immediately to God's people" (*Letter*, 73, 2).

Pope John Paul II stressed these same principles about Scripture interpretation in an address to the members of the Biblical Commission. He noted with satisfaction the progress being made in modern Catholic biblical scholarship since the encyclical *Providentissimus* written by Pope Leo XIII in 1893. He cited the many forms of scientific analysis of Scripture which have developed, such as the study of literary forms, semiotics, and narrative analysis.

He dwelt on the "limitations" of the new methods and asked his listeners to avoid the excesses of the swings of fashion in Scripture interpretation, for example, one school totally preoccupied with history and another one forgetting history altogether. He also advised his audience to observe the one-sidedness of some interpreters of Scripture such as those who cite Vatican II's document on Scripture (*Dei Verbum*) in support of the use of scientific methods, but seem to forget the other teaching of the council that interpreters should never forget the divine authorship of the Bible.

His next words deserve to be quoted in full:

The Bible has certainly been written in human language. Its interpretation requires the methodical use of the science of language. But it is also God's Word. Exegesis (Scripture interpretation) would be seriously incomplete if it did not shed light on the theological significance of Scripture.

We must not forget that Christian exegesis is a theological discipline, a deepening of the faith. This entails an interior tension between historical research founded on verifiable facts and research in the spiritual order based on faith in Christ. There is a great temptation to eliminate this inner tension by renouncing one or another of these two orientations . . . to be content with a subjective interpretation which is wrongly called "spiritual," or a scientific interpretation which makes the texts "sterile."

—English Edition of *L'Osservatore Romano*, April 22, 1991

This commentary/meditation which you are about to read was

written with this total vision in mind. You will not find it heavily scientific because it was not meant to be a popularization of the scientific methods of interpretation. At the same time, it is meant to reflect the beneficial results of scientific studies. You will discover it is aimed at opening up the person, message, and work of Jesus Christ whose work of salvation in union with the Father and the Holy Spirit is presented. Therefore, Jesus centered and faith growth envisioned.

It is my hope that these reflections will draw you to love the Bible, and in so doing, love Christ, yourself, and others. We are thus loving more than a book or sacred texts, we are in a total love affair. Perhaps Chaim Potok's description of the "Dance of the Torah" has something to say to us here. The scene is a Hasidic Synagogue in the Williamsburg section of Brooklyn. A religious festival is in progress and the participants have reached a part of the ceremony where scrolls of the Torah are passed around and certain privileged members are allowed to dance with it. We pick up the scene as the principal character, who has been agonizing about his faith and its relation to life, is handed the scroll.

> I held the scroll as something precious to me, a living being with whose soul I was forever bound, this Sacred Scroll, this Word, this Fire of God, this Source for my own creation, this velvet encased Fountain of All Life which I now clasped in a passionate embrace. I danced with the Torah for a long time, following the line of dancers through the steamy air of the synagogue and out into the chill tumultuous street and back into the synagogue and then reluctantly yielding the scroll to a huge dark-bearded man who hungrily scooped it up and swept away with it in his arms.
>
> —*The Gift of Asher Lev*, paperback, p. 351

Should not our encounter with Scripture be a dance with the Holy Word?

There was an old folk custom, now lost in the mists of history, in which a child was formally introduced to the sweetness of the Word of God. A page of the Bible was given to the child. Upon the page was spread some honey and the child was asked to taste it. Hence from earliest youth, the child would be introduced to a positive experience of Scripture, the sweetness of the Word of God.

What else need be said?

"How sweet are thy words to my taste,
sweeter than honey to my mouth."

—Ps. 119:103, RSV

Introduction

In April 1991, I made a pilgrimage to Lvov, Ukraine to be present at the first Catholic Easter liturgy to be celebrated in St. Yuri's cathedral in 43 years. On Holy Saturday at fifteen minutes before midnight, we lit our candles and left the cathedral. We went in procession around the building under the light of a new moon. Returned to the front, we found the door was closed. The deacon sang the Easter Gospel. When he came to the words, "Why look you for the living among the dead? He is risen! He is not here!" the celebrant sang out in a loud voice in Slavic, "Christos Voskrese!" (Christ is risen). We responded with equal vigor, "Voistinu Voskrese!" (He is risen indeed).

The doors opened and the huge crowd flowed into the cathedral for a joyous celebration of Easter. It was the first time in my life that I was at a liturgy where history and liturgy so perfectly coincided. Liturgically, we celebrated the resurrection of the Body of Jesus. Historically, we rejoiced in the resurrection of millions of members of the Body of Christ who had risen from the tomb of oppression and were now free to profess their faith openly. History and mystery touched each other. Amid the candles, incense, music, and palpable faith of the people there was a foretaste of heaven.

Such is the kind of feeling we will have as we enter the "cathedral" of John's gospel. The mystery of Easter permeates every page of his loving memoir of Jesus. In his pages we will encounter the Christ of glory.

I met a priest in Russia who had spent a year at the Zagorsk monastery. I asked him how he learned to be a spiritual man. He said, "I met a group of monks who practice the resurrection spirituality of John's gospel." For St. John, the light of Easter illumines the ministry of the earthly Jesus, revealing the hidden glory of the Word become flesh. It is like taking a journey going in an easterly direction at sunrise. The light of the sun reveals where we have been in our walk through the night.

This perspective enables us to see the spiritual purpose of the words and deeds of Jesus. Here the miracles are called signs. They are still events of kindness and compassion, but their threefold spiritual meaning is emphasized.

    (1). They are signs that help us experience the glory-presence of Jesus the Word become flesh.

   .(2). They are invitations to a faith relationship with Jesus.

    (3). They are powerful images of the Sacraments of Baptism and the Eucharist where such a relationship can occur.

The Wine miracle at Cana is more than a solution for the embarrassment of a young couple at a village wedding. The Bread miracle on the mountain transcends the satisfaction of a temporary hunger. These are signs that reveal how the risen Jesus ministers to us in the Eucharistic celebration.

Similarly, the words of Jesus here are mostly dialogues in which Jesus lovingly engages himself with others to bring them lasting happiness. He approaches people with sympathy and love and asks for personal union with them. With sure sensitivity he brings the Woman at the Well out of her loneliness and into a spiritual relationship with him that fills her with exuberant joy. With a similar empathy, he involves himself with Nicodemus, sowing the first seeds of faith-courage in him and sealing a relationship that matures at Calvary. The fearful Nicodemus becomes a public disciple of Jesus and assists in the burial.

Along the way, in these dialogues, we learn how the risen Jesus serves us in the Sacrament of Baptism. That is the point of the discussions about being born again of water and the Spirit, of water as an earthly sign of eternal life and love, of faith as a form of loving union with Jesus. Just as effectively, Jesus used the dialogue method in the Bread of Life discourse and his Last Supper conversations to show how he relates dynamically to us in our Eucharistic celebration.

Jesus is very personal and alive in this gospel. He insistently links his divine glory to his earthly identity and ministry. Thus he expresses his remarkable ability to reach out, not just to those in Capernaum, Galilee and Jerusalem, but to all of us in our present circumstances. Constantly, he uses the expression, I AM. God revealed himself as I AM to Moses at the burning bush. Jesus repeatedly applies the expression to himself in this gospel. It encompasses the seamless union of the Son of God and the son of Mary.

The I AM statements link Jesus with Light, Life, Way, Truth,

Shepherd, and Living Bread. He personalizes all these terms. His teaching is never abstract or disengaged from his listeners. He is the living embodiment of which he speaks. He shares himself with people, not because he has a need to talk about himself, but in order to give people the love, freedom, joy, truth, life, and forgiveness for which their hearts hunger.

Another term which illustrates Christ's enthusiastic yearning to have a personal impact on those he meets is "glory." In the Old Testament the glory was described as a pillar of fire or a shimmering cloud which rested on the Ark of the Covenant. Glory was like a sunrise in the morning or a fire in the sky at night. The Hebrews experienced God's presence in the glory of the pillar of fire that led them through the desert and the shining cloud over the Ark. The essential point was presence, God's wish to be intimate with his people.

This gospel says that Christ's miracle-signs manifested his glory. Jesus wanted to be as personally present to people as was possible. His presence included his human identity which was evident to them. But his love for them impelled him to share the fullness of his identity as the Word become flesh. Those who would behold him in faith would be in touch with the glory-presence of his divinity. That is why he kept pushing their awarenesses, their horizons to see more than their first impressions gave them. He did not do this out of any need to absorb their attention in him, so much as to accomplish his purpose of helping them to see what wonders he could fulfill in them. Just as the sun helps us to see what is in the world, the Word become flesh is our spiritual sunlight, enabling us to see what is possible within ourselves.

A word must be said here about this gospel and our Jewish brothers and sisters. Wrongly, some Christians have used some of its texts to justify anti-semitism. Vatican II has opposed anti-semitism and any attempt to use the Scripture to justify it. "Even though the Jewish authorities and those who followed their lead pressed for the death of Christ (see Jn. 19:6), neither all Jews indiscriminately at that time, nor Jews today, can be charged with crimes committed during his passion. . . . Remembering her common heritage with the Jews and moved not by any political consideration, but solely by the religious motivation of Christian charity, she deplores all hatreds, persecutions, displays of anti-semitism leveled at any time or from any source against the Jews" ("Non-Christian Religions," 4)[*].

We will find in this gospel that Christ's attitude is always in the best interests of others. He reaches out to Judas to help him change. He argues with religious leaders, not just to score debating points, but to bring them to light and love. He looks at the denying Peter with such compassion that the apostle weeps for his sins. He presses Pilate to discover his own inner hunger for truth. On the cross he says he thirsts for all people to accept his love and forgiveness. Never does he incite revenge, hatred, discrimination, or vindictiveness.

Easter is the best perspective for meditating on this gospel. The glory of the Risen Jesus, the Word become flesh, is the presence we will feel in its pages. Tradition says that St. John wrote this gospel at Ephesus and that Mary the mother of Jesus lived with him there. Her faith from the Annunciation to Ephesus was an arc of light, a rainbow. Her final years at Ephesus were a contemplative time. Jesus had said to her, "Behold, your son." From her contemplative depth, she could behold John composing this extraordinary gospel. Her motherly affection and her incomparable prayer touched her spiritual son. Since she is our mother too, she, who was present at the creation of this text, should be invoked for our own meditations.

Seat of Wisdom,
Pray for us.

---

[*]"Non-Christian Religions," *Nostra Aetate, Vatican Council II: Conciliar and Post Conciliar Documents*, Austin Flannery, ed. (Northport, NY: Costello Publishing Co., 1981).

1   In Peaceful Silence, Came the Almighty Word

The Canticle of the Word — The Prologue (Jn. 1:1-18)

The Christian assembly is singing in the prologue of John's gospel. This most exalted of gospels begins with a liturgical hymn that celebrates the divine origin of Jesus of Nazareth, the Word become flesh. We cannot hear the notes of their music, but we can definitely feel the faith.

So filled with the Spirit were those first Christians that they expressed their faith in a song that is one of the purest expressions of the meaning of Jesus of Nazareth that has ever been composed. In our imagination we can stand with John, the son of Zebedee, in the Christian assembly at Ephesus and look at his face as he sang this song with his fellow worshipers. When the Spirit moved him to write his gospel, he could think of no better way to begin this incomparable record of revelation than to use this prayerful poetry, which expressed the faith and worship of the church of his time.

Luke gave us the human face of Jesus as the privileged access to his divinity. John presents us with the divine identity of Jesus as the royal opening to appreciating his humanity. In each case we encounter the full mystery of Jesus.

Ingeniously, this liturgical hymn employed the image of the Word to unfold the mystery of Jesus. The Christian community of John the Beloved found a way to praise Jesus in an image that appealed both to its Jewish and Greek members. The Hebrew Scriptures personalized the Word as Divine Wisdom. Hence the Jews were already accustomed to thinking of the Word in personal terms. Greek philosophy maintained that the Word (or Logos) accounted for the inner dynamism of the world. Thus the Greeks connected the Word with reason as the impersonal force that ordered the world. Both Jews and Greeks linked the Word with creation. That is why the first words of the hymn repeat the first words of the Bible: "In the beginning." A second creation has begun.

Genesis taught that in the beginning, God created the world by speaking. "Then God said, 'Let there be light' " (Gn. 1:3). The Father created all humans, animals and the cosmos itself through his Word. John's gospel repeats this truth but amplifies the Genesis message by being more explicit. The Word was more than speech. The Word was God.

This Word generates and energizes all life. In the case of human beings, this life contains a potential for participation in divine life itself. In biblical thought God breathed life into each person, hence a human shimmers with an image of divinity already. But a person needs the ability to see this and embark on a journey to union with the divine.

That is why the Word — "The true light which enlightens everyone" (verse 9) — who endows us with the beginning of life is also our light to help us see our origins and our destiny. We need the light of the Word to appreciate the life received from the Word. The first gift of creation in Genesis is light. Throughout John's gospel, Jesus will return frequently to these basic themes of life and light.

Sin causes us to walk in darkness. It blunts our awareness of the exciting truths proclaimed here. Sin makes us forget our true identity. It places our origin and destiny in the shadows. Many people feel this shadow when they try to look into themselves. The shadow is the evidence of the darkness, for which the ultimate cure is the light of the Word, Jesus Christ. His light still shines despite the shadows. The darkness will never overcome his light. Historically, that victory has been won by the death and resurrection of Jesus. Personally, we can share in that victory through faith and baptism, grace, and continual moral conversion.

John the evangelist inserts here in verses 6-8 a note about John the Baptist, sent from God to draw people's attention to Jesus Christ, to invite them to believe in him who is the true light of the world. This observation eliminates any ambiguity about who the Word is. The Word is the Son of God, Jesus Christ.

After this clarification, the hymn resumes with the theme of light. Our rational culture makes us think of the light as intellectual illumination, something that comes from the process of logic and thinking. But the light of the Word is not first seen by a clever mind, or arrived at by extensive thinking, however sincere or deep. Reason can only deduce the existence of God. Love, expressed as faith, experiences the personal presence of the Word. Love alone has the eyes that perceive the Word. Love knows more than the Word's existence. Love knows the presence. Then the Word is known as light. The fourth gospel frequently speaks of the union of faith and love (Jn. 6:66-69; 11:20-27; 20:1-8; 21:7).

Mother Teresa tells a story about visiting an old man in a dark and dirty room. She wanted to clean it up for him, but at first he refused. After she gained his trust, he let her clean it. She found a lamp crusted with dust and asked him why he never lit it. He told her that there was no reason to do so because no one came to see him. Would he light it if her sisters visited him? He agreed. "If I hear a human voice I will light it." She heard later that now his lamp is lit all the time. Affection leads to the light.

The Word is light because the Word is Love. First our hearts see the Word. Then our minds form thoughts about the Word.

This gospel says the world failed to recognize the Word. Even many of his own people did not accept him. But some did and they were given power to be the children of God and believe in his name. Their union with divine Love did not come from merely being born. Nor was it caused by a human choice based on logic and common sense. They chose union with the divine Word-Love because Love first chose them.

They were open and ready for this because they had a purity and simplicity of heart which made this possible. Or in other instances their sinfulness and feeling of being lost caused them to hunger for love and forgiveness. They sought the light and found Jesus.

The Word became flesh and lived among us in a human community. A Christmas antiphon says, "When the sun rises in the morning sky, you will see the King of Kings coming forth from the Father like a bridegroom from a bridal chamber." The Word who was the brightness of the Father's glory came to us in a body of flesh. The Word did this for us so we could share in his holiness, to make us partakers of the divine life, to plant the seed of absolute Love in our hearts.

The Word Becomes Flesh

Christian realism has strenuously affirmed the incarnation of the Word by using as basic a term as one can employ, flesh. From the very beginning there were people who tried to separate the Word from flesh. Greek philosophy sought liberation from the material world and the burdens of the flesh. It could not imagine God taking a body.

Christians replied that the Word did not just live inside a body, like God wearing a costume, as that philosophy maintained. Truly, "The Word became flesh" (Jn. 1:14). Jesus the Word liberated us from sin while honoring the positive aspects of the flesh and the material world. He showed us how the body and creation can be a stage on which to sing God's praises in innocence and purity. The Word became flesh and entered into human history.

When peaceful silence lay over all,
and night had run half of her swift course,
down from the heavens, from the royal throne
leapt your all-powerful Word.

—Wis. 18:14-15 Jerusalem Bible

At the same time the Word never ceased to be God. Godhead and manhood are joined together in One Person — the Word. The Son of God took our human nature truly and authentically, "like us in all things but sin." Meditative people throughout history have offered various ways of appreciating this deep mystery. In the end, the faith of the church and personal meditation and the disclosures that come from loving union with Jesus, give the best access to the reality of the Word. Light from Jesus, when communicated in a loving exchange, helps us see his glory.

"And we saw his glory, the glory as of the Father's only Son, full of grace and truth" (Jn. 1:14).

The Jesus "Glory"

To understand the meaning of the term glory here, we should look at how the expression was used in the Old Testament. Glory is the biblical way of speaking of God's presence. The people of the Hebrew covenant said they experienced God's presence in terms of majesty, power, the glow of his holiness, the dynamism of his being. Many scriptural texts speak of glory as God's presence, as in the liberation at the Red Sea, the appearance of the manna, and even in storms. Isaiah exclaimed that the glory made him feel God's presence with the vividness and intimacy of cloth against the skin (Is. 6:1).

God manifested his glory as light, warmth, guidance, surprise, everywhereness, and the source of our self discovery. God as pillar of cloud and fire illustrated his presence that lit up the world of the Hebrews and guided them. God's glory as breath and air spoke of his presence to all creation. The glory of God resting on the ark in the vision of Isaiah was a cause of religious conversion for him. The burning bush did this for Moses and whirling suns caused a similar experience for Ezekiel. God came with his powerful presence in these signs, personally changing these men.

This glory is an act of personal presence. God as glory is God seeking a communion with each of us. It is God present to us for the purpose of influencing our awareness and desires with his creative, transforming and redeeming love. Hence biblical people did not stare at the glory of God, but experienced in the core of their hearts the fire of divine love and presence.

They were doing more than gazing at the equivalent of a glorious sunrise. They were feeling within themselves the most pleasant experience available to a human being, the inner approach of one who would totally and convincingly fulfill their most basic longings.

The Great Hymn in John's prologue gathers up all these diverse experiences of God's glory in the Hebrew covenant. It declares that Jesus is the Son of that God whose glory and faithfulness Israel came to know. Jesus now possesses exactly that same glory. God's love and truth was enfleshed in a real, historical human being whom people could see, hear, and touch. To see his glory now meant being in a growing personal relationship with him who affected their entire lives with a love that thrilled, challenged, forgave, and changed them forever.

Jesus the Word is full of grace and truth. The words grace and truth were frequently applied to God in the Old Testament. Grace meant God's transforming kindness, affection, and love. Truth meant more than an abstract statement of a principle or a standard. Truth implied fidelity, as in the saying, "This above all, to thine own self be true."

Just as God was full of transforming kindness (grace) and fidelity (truth) so also was Jesus who treats us with the fullness of a kind and faithful person. When we experience the glory of the Word, we encounter love and fidelity in its absolute form. When the spark of a relationship is struck between Jesus and us, then we begin to finally know what it is like to be changed by someone who truly loves us and will never let us down.

As the music and poetry of this Great Hymn settle into our

awareness, we are drawn to a lifelong relationship with Jesus. This is less a time for analysis and more an occasion for letting ourselves be loved and responding with affection. Then we acclaim what the final surge of the hymn tells us, "From his fullness, we have all received" (verse 16).

Desert Voice (Jn. 1:19-34)

As the splendor of the Great Hymn receded, the affairs of daily life resumed. The gospel focuses on the role of John the Baptist. His activity is best understood against the background of Old Testament prophecy. Four hundred years before the birth of Christ, there had been an era of prophets, stretching back several centuries. In various ways they foretold the coming of the messiah. In the next four hundred years the voice of prophecy was silent.

Then came John the Baptist, looking and sounding like the mighty prophets of old. Practicing a desert spirituality, he passed countless hours alone in silence, communing with God. His powerful spiritual lifestyle inspired numerous moral conversions. People listened with respect to his words because his personal life was so clearly and honestly spiritual. He preached moral conversion with the fervor of an Elijah. He cited the rich poetry of Isaiah to alert people that the messiah's arrival was imminent.

With messianic expectations newly aroused, the religious leaders approached the Baptist to ask him if he were the messiah himself. Or Elijah? Or the prophet? They mentioned Elijah because of the popular belief that he had to come back again and finish his life cycle, and that he would do this in messianic times. Recall that Elijah had not died a proper death, but was borne into the skies in a fiery chariot and not seen or heard from again. The "prophet" of whom they spoke, referred to a prediction of Moses that "A prophet like me will the Lord raise up for you" (Dt. 18:15). Folk religion assumed that Jeremiah was most like Moses and that he was the one to look for in messianic times. Since the Baptist acted a lot like Jeremiah, it was natural to think he was fulfilling this prophecy.

The Baptist told them he was not the messiah, nor Elijah, nor the prophet. He was a desert voice urging people to undertake the spiritual renewal necessary to recognize and welcome the messiah. His baptisms at the Jordan were a first stage in this spiritual readiness. His baptism helped people wash away their old attitudes and worn out ways of thinking. The bath in the Jordan symbolized their decision to cleanse their hearts of immoral desires and their behavior of sinful practices.

The messiah will also baptize with water, but will go further. He will introduce the creative power of God's breath or Spirit. The messiah's baptism would have the force of creation, making a new woman and a new man out of the recipient. When the God of Genesis combined his breath-Spirit with the waters, a creation occurred. John's baptism with water simply produced an improved person. Christ's creative baptism would generate a truly *new* person.

The next day the Baptist told his disciples what he believed about Jesus. Like the great prophets of the Golden Age, the Baptist attracted disciples. As their spiritual master, the Baptist would have initiated them into desert spirituality. He invited them into the great silences of the desert, taught them how to survive on very simple foods, and to let the mystery of God enfold them.

He also shared with them his Spirit-inspired belief that the messianic moment had arrived. He went further and named his cousin Jesus as that very person. They had seen him baptize Jesus and then watch Christ go off, just as they did, alone into the desert. They were veterans of this mighty solitude and also retained the memories of the spiritual battles they experienced as they confronted themselves in their self-imposed isolation. They knew something of what was in store for Jesus and wondered how he would emerge from his first known days in the desert.

Possibly it was forty days later, while they were gathered for a teaching from their master, they saw Jesus coming out of the desert (verse 29). They recognized the lean look. They also beheld the warmth that tempered his austere appearance, for the Spirit who brought him there stayed with him throughout the challenging days. They would hear that angels came and consoled him after the conquest of Satan. Jesus looked ready to begin a mysterious mission.

The Baptist raised his arms in welcome and said of his cousin that he was the lamb of God who would take away the sin of the world. By using the expression "lamb," the Baptist aroused in his listeners the picture of the servant of Isaiah 53. Like a lamb this servant-martyr was sacrificed that by his sufferings the wound of people's sins would be healed.

Another rich connection came from the story of the sacrifice of Isaac, where the young man asked his father Abraham, "Who shall provide the lamb?" Abraham replied that God would give the lamb. As the Baptist warmly embraced his cousin, he gave his followers the look that said, "God has given us the lamb in this man." Jesus is the ultimate servant-martyr who has come to redeem us.

What would this lamb/person do? He would take away the world's sin. No one could be more conscious of the reality of sin than the Baptist and his desert community. The lonely spiritual struggles each of them had fought in the spare vastness around them had given them an exceptional awareness of the evil drives that arose from their inner depths. They were not naive about their potential sinfulness. They faced moral reality. They did not deny it or lose themselves in illusions that would persuade them there was no moral order.

One purpose of their spiritual disciplines was to cleanse their hearts of sinful desires and their behavior of sinful acts. The baptist now tells them that Jesus the lamb would deliver them from sin. He said no more than that. He did not describe how that would happen. But by using a sacrificial symbol, he taught them that Jesus would somehow be sacrificed so they could experience salvation.

The Baptist then said something strange. Twice he said that he did not recognize Jesus. Obviously he did know Jesus from early childhood. As cousins they grew up together, playing, eating, singing, joining in family birthdays, weddings, funerals, and other gatherings. Who knows what secrets they shared and what spiritual influences they exerted on each other? All of that the Baptist definitely knew. So why does he say he did not know Jesus?

He means that he did not know, until his baptism of Jesus, the extraordinary truth about him. At the Jordan baptism he received a revelation about Jesus. He beheld the Spirit hovering like a dove over Jesus. In biblical imagery, the dove symbolized the end of the flood to Noah and God's reconciliation with the world. A new creation began with the survivors of the ark. John saw the Spirit/dove anoint Jesus as the source of a new spiritual creation and prepared him to be the ultimate reconciler of all humans with God.

That moment of revelation returned as he gazed on his beloved cousin and intimate friend. The Spirit filled the Baptist again and moved him to a further prophetic utterance (see verse 33). John said that Jesus will baptize with the Holy Spirit as well as water. And then possessed even more strongly with divine insight, the Baptist said: "Now I have seen and have testified that he is the Son of God" (verse 34).

Disciple Selection (Jn. 1:35-51)

The next day, Jesus began selecting his disciples. His first candidates came from the Baptist's circle of followers. Their names were John and Andrew. They addressed him as Rabbi and asked where he was staying. Jesus said, "Come and see." This is a call to discipleship. "Come and see" is an invitation to follow a person first of all. People will listen to teachers only when they are impressed with the witness of the teacher. Jesus called the apostles to experience him as a person and to observe his witness. Then his teachings would begin to sink in. The witness gives the credibility.

Andrew's call was a life changing encounter for him. He would never be quite the same again. Till his dying day he would even recall the hour it happened, 4 p.m. (verse 39). Andrew was so taken with Jesus that he went and recruited his brother Simon to join their little group. Andrew told him they had found the messiah. When Jesus met Simon, he changed his name to Peter, which means rock.

The following day Jesus encountered Philip and said, "Follow me." Philip came from Bethsaida, the town of Andrew and Peter. Philip went to his friend Nathanael and told him he had found the one that Moses and the prophets had written about, Jesus of Nazareth. Nathanael wondered if anybody worthwhile could come from Nazareth. Philip said, "Come and see."

When Jesus met Nathanael he said that here was a man in whom there was no duplicity. Nathanael asked him how could he tell that since he never saw him before. Jesus said that he had seen him under a fig tree before Philip ever invited him to join their group. Nathanael became effusive and declared, "You are the *Son of God*. You are the *King of Israel*."

This narrative of the call of the apostles shows how important personal contact was in bringing someone to Jesus. At the same time, it demonstrates that Jesus does the choosing. Lastly, this text combines the calling stories with a series of faith statements about Jesus. They call him Rabbi, messiah, Son of God, and King of Israel. The author of the fourth gospel tells us from the very first chapter who Jesus of Nazareth is, from Word become flesh to all the other designations heard from the lips of the apostles. He expresses the full faith of the church about Jesus, even though for the disciples and the early church their growth in understanding Jesus before the resurrection was more gradual. In the remainder of the gospel all these truths will be visibly demonstrated in the message and ministry of Jesus.

Reflection

1. How have I best experienced the human side of Jesus?
2. How have I known the divine mystery of Jesus?
3. The Word as light is best perceived through a loving faith. What does it mean to say my heart will know the Word and then my mind will form words about what my heart perceives?
4. If the Word is the source of my whole life, what does that say about my spiritual goals?
5. Why did the Word become flesh?
6. What words might I use to share my faith in the Word made flesh?
7. What did the Baptist mean when he said he did not *know* Jesus?
8. The Baptist and his followers practiced desert spirituality, seeking solitude and silence to be open to God. How might I practice something like that today?
9. When I hear Jesus called "lamb" what occurs to me?
10. What will this first chapter mean for my spiritual life?

Prayer

Word become flesh, I adore you and thank you for your great love which motivated you to become one of us to save us. I am filled with awe by this mystery. Grant me the gift of gratitude and the faith that will help me respond to your affection so magnificently given to me and the world. Shine within my heart every moment of my days and nights.

2   A Day of Wine — A Night of Glory

A Wedding and a Wine Miracle (Jn. 2:1-11)

Wednesdays were the preferred days for weddings. The Mishna, a collection of oral laws, established the rule about Wednesday weddings. In all probability the marriage feast at Cana was the customary midweek celebration. The bride and groom would have vowed themselves to one another under a wedding canopy — a reminder that in nomadic times this ceremony took place in a tent. Flowing wine cheered the hearts of the guests.

The gospel says the mother of Jesus was there. Oddly, this gospel never refers to her name, Mary, even though she appears in two of its most powerful scenes, Cana and the cross. Her prominent role at this wedding suggests she may have been a close relative of either the bride or groom. This may also account for the presence of Jesus.

Soon after his arrival, Mary told him there was no wine left. It is not clear how this embarrassing situation arose. Some have guessed it may have been caused by Jesus' new disciples, seven unexpected guests. This assumes they brought no wine gifts, most likely because they had no opportunity to purchase any.

Regardless of the cause, the crisis was real and Mary sought a solution. Apparently, nothing short of a miracle could solve the problem. Presumably, local village wine supplies had been exhausted. Or the family had no money left to buy more. The statement that preceded the forthcoming wine miracle ("They have no wine") is similar to that which introduced the bread miracle in the feeding of the five thousand ("They have no bread"). They have nothing to drink at Cana and they have nothing to eat in the wilderness.

In church history, Mary is our honored intercessor for divine favors. Already at Cana, acting as intercessor, she asked Jesus to help this bewildered couple and their families. We should remember that between Mary and her son there existed a bond, not just of an ordinary mother and an exceptionally devoted son, but that of a believer and a disciple. Her faith in her son began with her consent to conceive him. Her cousin Elizabeth had praised her for her religious faith.

For over thirty years the most remarkable relationship on earth had matured in the little village of Nazareth. Mary was the responsible mother raising a boy and guiding him into manhood. She was also contemplating the extraordinary mystery of her beloved Jesus. Her deep silences and prayers accompanied her instructions, laughter, tears, conversations, nursings, and whatever else it took to raise him. None of the busy-ness of being his mother would ever still the wonder in her heart. Seconds, minutes, hours, and years chronicled the sturdy advance of her faith. No relationship between a mother and son should ever be trivialized. In the case of Mary and her son, it would be reckless to do so.

Jesus proved to be the dutiful son. He obeyed her and grew in wisdom, age, and grace before all. While it is graceless to probe where Scripture itself remains silent, it is legitimate to say that Jesus was a loving and caring son. And it does not seem out of place to observe that in his communion with Mary, he revealed his inner self little by little through his everyday actions. If Mary's faith burned like a clear star, her son's self disclosure opened to her like the warmth of the sun.

The term "mystery" in Scripture means both something hidden and something revealed. Mystery is the unknown to be made known. The infinite mystery of Jesus can never be completely known. On the other hand, Jesus is not shrouded in thick darkness, so that his inner self can never be experienced. He is the "light" after all.

We hear a great deal today about the value of dialogue and interpersonal communion. That is exactly what went on between Mary and Jesus for the thirty years prior to this hour at Cana. No Carmelite nun or Trappist monk has ever testified to having a deeper appreciation of Jesus than Mary did, even after their own thirty years of loving contemplation. In fact they claim they have only begun to taste the mystery of Jesus and are filled with what they call a "holy envy" of the faith of Mary.

It is perhaps no accident that this gospel places Mary in the center of things just after the call of the disciples. She is not only the mother of Jesus, but also his first and best disciple, for her call came three decades before from the lips of the angel Gabriel. She was both the teaching mother and the learning disciple.

This reflection about her relationship to Jesus puts into perspective the dialogue between them at Cana. Theirs is a communion so deep that the words on the gospel page should be matched by the unsaid words, the signals based on heart understandings rooted in thirty years of mutual exchange.

On the surface Mary seems to be asking nothing more than a practical favor, an act of simple charity to this distressed couple. At another level she is encouraging him to begin publicly his work of salvation. At the Jordan, the heavenly Father commissioned Jesus to salvation ministry. At Cana, the earthly mother released him from home life and urged him to start his active ministry.

This clarifies Christ's enigmatic response to her. Jesus completely understood what she meant. Their communion as son and mother assured that outcome. His use of the word "hour" indicated a temporary hesitation about beginning his ministry. He is not talking about "clock time" but about the right, suitable, and appropriate time, what the Greeks called "kairos." Had Jesus concluded Mary was simply asking him a pragmatic favor, such as going out and trying to buy more wine, he would not have responded with messianic language about his "hour."

If this were only a matter of solving a family problem, Jesus would not have addressed her as "woman." Had he called her mother, he would have spoken of her physical parentage. By addressing her as "woman" he elevated her to a maternal role in the history of salvation. He spoke to her motherhood in the spirit, not just in the flesh. She would be concerned with the range of all human needs, but above all for the salvation of every man and woman.

Hence Christ's words to Mary, which seem abrupt and even unfilial to us, are in fact a confirmation of her spiritual motherhood. The Christ light had shone on her faith and revealed to her the spiritual destiny that lay before her. The future beckoned her to open her maternal heart to all people. Nor was this a vague and fuzzy kind of call. It was specific and concrete. Decisively, Mary goes to the wine steward and tells him, "Do whatever he tells you" (verse 5).

There were six water jars for ceremonial washings. Jesus told the servants to fill them with water. Each jar could hold twenty gallons. Jesus then instructed the servants to draw out some from the jars and take that to the headwaiter. When he tasted the water that became wine, he was astonished. He said that people usually serve the best wine first and then an inferior one after people had drunk copiously. In this case the best wine was saved for last. The fearful bride and groom need worry no more. The guests could enjoy themselves with 120 gallons of the finest wine.

This was the first sign by which Jesus would reveal his glory, his inner divinity, and call for faith from those who witnessed his action. The gospel says that from this moment, his disciples began to believe in him. They took the first tentative steps on their journey of faith. To them he was no longer just an impressive Rabbi, but someone who elicited from them the kind of faith they usually reserved for God.

The Cana miracle was the first of seven miracles — or signs — recorded in John's gospel. Here is a list of them.

1. The Wine Miracle 2:1-11
2. Cure of the Nobleman's Son 4:46-54
3. Healing the Impotent Man 5:2-9
4. The Bread Miracle 6:4-13
5. Walking on water 6:16-21
6. The Man Born Blind 9:1-41
7. Raising of Lazarus 11:1-44

John calls these events signs rather than miracles to emphasize that the miracles always had a religious purpose beyond their human uses. Each of the seven signs was a call to faith in the total person of Jesus. The wine miracle had its human goal, namely, to alleviate the anxiety of the wedding hosts. It also had a divine purpose — to challenge people to see the glory revealed by Jesus and respond with faith commitment to him. All seven sign-miracles in John have this same dual outcome, a human benefit and an invitation to a faith surrender to Jesus.

In our meditation on the Great Hymn in chapter one, we explored what it means to say one beholds the "glory" of the Word. We emphasized that it is a way of speaking about the Word of God's presence and our experience of that personal approach of the divine. This movement of the Word to make his presence felt in our lives is more than just getting acquainted. The Word has a greater interest in us than simply dropping by for a visit and killing time, however pleasantly. Jesus, the Word, wants to be present to us in such a way that he influences our awareness and desires with the force of his transforming love.

This happened at Cana. His wine miracle doubtless astonished his disciples. Amazing them, however, was not enough. Stunning people simply leaves them with their mouths open. Being wholly present to them with a love that is irresistible leaves them with an open heart. The glory of Jesus, which glowed that evening at Cana amid the smiles of a spring night, the abandon of youthful dancers and the joy of hearts warmed by the best wine ever drunk, probed deeply into the souls of his new disciples and insisted on a rush of faith. The gospel says they began to believe at that hour.

The wine miracle contains three other Christian teachings. First, it announces the arrival of messianic times. The wedding party had 120 gallons of wine, the equivalent of nearly 500 bottles. Such abundance recalled the prophecy of Amos that in the era of the messiah, rivers of wine would flow in the Judean hills. "The juice of grapes shall drip down the mountains, and all the hills shall run with it" (Amos 9:13).

Second, it argues that the most stable source of ecstasy is union with Jesus. This is why the liturgy of early Christianity chose the Cana story as one of the readings for January 6th, the feast of the Epiphany. Greek pagan religion had used that date to celebrate the festival of Dionysus, the god of wine. On some wealthy estates, wine flowed from the water fountains to mark the feast.

The pagan holiday legitimized public intoxication and socially approved drunkenness. This alcohol induced ecstasy repelled Christians because of its orgiastic outcomes and its dehumanizing effects. The use of God's gift of wine had become an abuse. Christians did not disdain the prudent use of wine, but condemned its abuse. They replaced this dionysian frenzy with the restrained festival of the Epiphany — the manifestation of Christ's glory. The "wine" of Christ's Holy Spirit was a true and enduring source of human happiness.

Third, the Cana miracle symbolized the wine of the Holy Eucharist. This is the sacramental interpretation of the miracle. The Lord's Supper would be centered on the wine and the bread, the wine becoming his blood of the covenant and the bread becoming his body to be broken. The bread miracle of John 6 will balance this imagery at Cana.

The Cana story is a poem condensed into eleven verses. At first sight it seems to be little more than a charming tale of a village wedding. The couple faced an unexpected problem. A sympathetic family member asks her son to help them. By turning out to be a prophetic wonder worker, Jesus produces a surprising solution. But like all great poetry, the tightly packed words need to be unraveled. The genius of John was his ability to store in these few verses a deep revelation, which has become for us an immensely rich source for our faith reflection and development. To speak of this incident as poetry is not to question its history, but rather to insist that the history was related to us with the skill of a poet.

Jesus Purifies the Temple (Jn. 2:12-25)

It was Passover time, so Jesus went to Jerusalem to celebrate the feast at the temple. He found the sellers of oxen, sheep and doves marketing the sacrificial animals at prices far above the going rate. The temple officials had a monopoly on these animals which they claimed were the only ones suitable for sacrifice. Poorer people were trapped into buying from them rather than at more reasonable prices from other markets. To make matters worse, they could only use the temple currency, so they had to exchange their money for temple cash — and naturally had to pay a fee for the exchange.

This commercializing of the Passover sacrifices infuriated Jesus who made a whip of cords. Thus armed, he roared through the stalls, overthrowing the tables, spilling the money on the marble floors, and chasing the animals out of the enclosures and cages. He shouted at the owners that they were a disgrace, making his Father's house of prayer into a den of thieves. His radical behavior reminded his disciples of Jeremiah the prophet who had condemned these same practices centuries ago (Jer. 7:10). Seeing Christ's fury, they remembered the words of the psalmist: ". . . zeal for your house consumes me" (Ps. 69:10).

The temple rulers asked him what was the meaning of his action. Jesus said, "Destroy this temple and in three days I will raise it up" (verse 19). They replied that it took forty-six years to build it. How could he rebuild it in three days? This kind of exchange will happen many times in John. Commentators call it "Johannine irony." Someone asks a question at a purely natural level. Christ's answer is at a spiritual level. The questioner comes back with a literalistic response, missing Christ's point. Here, the gospel writer adds, after the misunderstanding of the rulers, that Jesus was talking about the temple of his body, not the stone and marble building before them.

The history of spiritual masters is full of similar teaching devices. Asian spiritual teachers use "koans," mysterious sayings that are meant to jolt the listeners out of their everyday perceptions, such as, "What is the sound of one hand clapping?" The reality of God is both very far away from ordinary perception, and at the same time intimately close. But the flow of daily preoccupations blinds us from experiencing God. Jesus would strive to break this self-limiting perception with his mysterious sayings. It is like shock therapy for the human spirit, shaking the listener into a flash of spiritual insight.

Jesus is doing more than scoring debating points. He is truly attempting to help the temple rulers escape from the religious routines which had stalled their spiritual development. It is the same for us. We have heard his saying about the temple of his body for many years. We assume we are more perceptive than the temple rulers because we know the gospel interpretation. Our challenge is to look at our own frozen perceptions, religious routines, and dispassionate approaches and see Jesus in a fresh and vital way.

Certain life experiences will awaken us from our spiritual lethargy. The birth of a child, the death of a spouse or other family member, an accident, a sudden illness, the loss of a job, a move to a new neighborhood, these are potential spiritual awakeners. They snap the predictable flow of our lives and induce reflection. If we are sufficiently alert, these teachable moments can put us in touch with the stillpoint deep within our souls where Jesus, the Word, the light seeks to influence our affectivity and attitudes.

Another ordinary way to escape the deadening force of routine is meditation time everyday where we surrender with sharp attention to the sounds of silence within our hearts. This daily discipline makes us remember we have an inner life that is just as real as the busy one outside. A regular journey into our inner selves puts us in touch with the dynamism of our souls and the light and love of Jesus. This constant exercise of our spiritual life makes our external moral, doctrinal, and liturgical behavior ring with vitality and undercuts the inertia that otherwise stalls us.

We all suffer from forgetfulness of being. We forget the vast inner world we carry around inside us and settle for the narrow, small, confining world of externals. It is too dark to interpret itself.

Only Jesus can light up this world of immediacy. An inner dialogue with him makes this possible.

Reflection

1. What did Jesus mean when he addressed his mother as "woman"?
2. What is the "hour" of which Jesus spoke?
3. In my own words, how would I speak of the faith relationship Mary had with Jesus during the thirty years prior to Cana?
4. If Mary said to me, "Do what ever Jesus tells you," what would that mean for my spiritual life?
5. What is one reason why the church chose January 6th for the feast of the Epiphany?
6. How does the wine miracle refer to the Eucharist?
7. What caused Jesus to cleanse the temple?
8. Why did Jesus use a mysterious saying in his dialogue with the temple administrators?
9. What do I need to jolt me out of my customary ways of thinking?
10. The New Testament says that our bodies are "Temples of the Holy Spirit." What should I do to make the "Temple of my body" a house of prayer?

Prayer

Jesus, at the Cana wedding you manifested your glory by your wine miracle. Your revelation of yourself initiated your disciples into their journey of faith in you. I also experience your revelation when I prayerfully meditate on these rich eleven verses. Jolt me from my staid ways of relating to you so I may grow in personal union with you. Transform me by your love.

3 God So Loved the World, That He Sent His Son

Dialogue With Nicodemus (Jn. 3:1-21)

Following is an imaginary conversation based on the text.

Nicodemus: I realize this is a late hour at night to meet with you. I frankly admit that I am reluctant to be seen in public with you. My colleagues at the Sanhedrin would not approve my positive attitude toward you.

Jesus: I don't have the credentials?

Nicodemus: Well, you have achieved the status of a rabbi without going through the formal, approved stages of discipleship like the rest of us.

Jesus: I'm not properly certified.

Nicodemus: You know what I mean. We are a jealous lot. We guard our positions and are possessive about our ranks.

Jesus: Do you really think your membership would be more comfortable with me if I had their rabbinic training?

Nicodemus: You're not making this easy for me.

Jesus: Perhaps I want you to be more honest about yourself.

Nicodemus: Is this secret night appointment bothering you?

Jesus: You seem to be the one who is uneasy.

Nicodemus: I have a family to care for and a position to maintain. I could be very useful to you.

Jesus: You are more in need of inner courage. You are too fearful.

Nicodemus: Believe me, I am a better man than I sound.

Jesus: Why have you come?

Nicodemus: You and I know that our religious tradition teaches us that God sometimes approves a rabbi's teachings by giving him the power to perform miracles.

Jesus: Yes.

Nicodemus: What I mean to say is. . . . Well, I have heard about your astonishing Cana miracle. People have reported other miracles.

Jesus: Which brings you to me tonight.

Nicodemus: I believe that you are a teacher sent from God.

Jesus: Why have you reached this conclusion?

Nicodemus: No one could do that unless God were with him.

Jesus: So you see me as a teacher, missioned by God.

Nicodemus: Yes.

Jesus: Nothing more?

Nicodemus: I don't know what you mean. I see you as a privileged teacher. You know it is a rare gift. You haven't gone through the steps that lead to an official rank as teacher. God has blessed you.

Jesus: Dear friend, I'm afraid you have much more to learn about me. You are limited by your traditional view of a wonder worker. Yes, I am a teacher from God, but I am a lot more than that. I am not merely teaching about the kingdom of God. I am bringing you the kingdom. I have come from God.

Nicodemus: How could I be expected to know that? I am not even sure I know what you are saying.

Jesus: You need to be born again from above.

Nicodemus: You continue to puzzle me. Am I to return to my mother's womb for a second birth?

Jesus: I am talking about your spiritual birth. You should permit God's Spirit to remake your mind and transform your whole nature. This will happen when you look deeply within yourself and notice how much change you need.

Nicodemus: I'm losing you.

Jesus: I'm inviting you to discover your inner life, to listen to your hungers and your hopes.

Nicodemus: If I do that, what will I find?

Jesus: That you yearn for change and personal growth in love.

Nicodemus: Let's say that I do. Am I to change myself?

Jesus: When your inner desire has recognized that only a divine power can change you, then you will know what I mean.

Nicodemus: And that is your teaching about being born from above?

Jesus: No one can enter the kingdom of God's transforming love without being born of water and the Holy Spirit.

Nicodemus: Why water? Why Spirit?

Jesus: Water here symbolizes your life in need of change and conversion. The waters of the first chapter of Genesis were lifeless and chaotic. Something like your inner life right now. Only when God's creative breath-Spirit permeated those waters did creation begin. I am describing an intimate encounter between you and divine Love.

Nicodemus: I thought water was a positive, cleansing agent.

Jesus: In spiritual matters it becomes so when united with the power of the Spirit.

Nicodemus: Your Spirit language bewilders me.

Jesus: Think of the wind. You know it exists. You feel it. You hear it. Yet you can't see it. There is something mysterious about it. Think of it as an image of God's Spirit. You can experience God's presence, but the mystery of God remains.

Nicodemus: How can all this be?

Jesus: You are the trained teacher, yet you do not know. You are good at explaining words, texts and teachings. You can quote authors and experts with ease. But you have let the words control you. The whole point of your teaching should be growth in faith in divine realities. You pay too much attention to the words and not enough to the divine speaker.

Nicodemus: How can you help me?

Jesus: Put some love into your life and some life into your love. Then you will awaken to the grandeur of God's plan. God has so loved you and everyone that he has sent his Son here so that everyone who believes in him might not perish, but have eternal life.

Nicodemus: I need time to take in all you have shared with me. You have touched me in a way I did not expect. Be assured I shall never forget this night.

Three Applications of This Dialogue

The twenty-one verses that chronicle the conversation between Jesus and Nicodemus contain rich spiritual teachings for our lives. The following three considerations, among many others, seem especially beneficial.

1. Put conversion first on the religious agenda. Nicodemus sought a theological discussion. Jesus invited him to conversion. Nicodemus liked teacher talk. Jesus insisted on personal commitment. Nicodemus wanted a meeting of minds. Jesus demanded a meeting of hearts. Nicodemus expected a lively rabbinic dissection of Scripture texts from someone who seemed to be an accomplished interpreter. Jesus upset his plans by involving him in a personal encounter. The Pharisee delighted in mental combat. The Master enjoyed explorations of the spirit. The Pharisee searched for answers. The Master confronted him with questions.

This does not imply that Jesus had no interest in religious doctrine. In fact he used the religious doctrine about the action of the Spirit to open up the soul of his visitor. But a discussion of religious doctrine as a mental exercise does little good unless the persons involved are already operating at a faith level. The implication here is that Nicodemus had put too much stock in the mental gymnastics associated with scriptural teachings.

Nicodemus was theologizing.

Jesus was evangelizing.

The lesson for ourselves is self evident. Even as we study the Scriptures, we can make study substitute for faith growth. We can tend to treat Scripture as a detective story in which we probe for solutions to fascinating literary and historical problems. Valuable as that is, it is not the primary purpose for approaching Scripture. We take up the word of God to meet the Word of God. We read the Bible to experience divine love. First we take the text into our hearts and only after that into our heads. Jesus was basically saying to Nicodemus, "I am not a book. I am a person." Please relate to me in my total personhood and you will find a love and fulfillment that is the real key to understanding the sacred Scripture.

When we have discovered this secret of entering into a lifelong conversion process, then we will find Scripture to be full of light for our lives. Our second consideration is about a way to do this.

2. Permit the Spirit's transforming influence. The Spirit of Jesus is always ready to meet us and influence our awareness and desires. But the Spirit will not affect us unless we freely choose to receive that influence. Scripture says that God is like a potter and we are the clay. The image of clay implies malleability, the capacity for being shaped. We must acquire a sense of inwardness where we experience the dynamism of our whole inner life, spiritual, psychic and mental.

Our culture favors us getting in touch with the psychological side of our inner life. We are nudged to examine our feelings — even to "feel our feelings." After that we are asked to analyze these emotions. That is all well and good and such an endeavor has its well known positive results.

In pre-psychological cultures, people tended to put greater stock in getting in touch with the intellect. Educated people spoke of the cultivation of the mind, of having a well-furnished mind. That culture prized a liberal arts education, believed that truth could be known and that ideas have consequences. That goal has not disappeared today, but it must compete with the intense preoccupation with inner emotions that attract so many now.

But there is a third component to our inner life and that is the spirit. Its action is something akin to intuition and the act of wonder. The human spirit is the inner faculty that is capable of having a personal relationship with God. Some people call this the stillpoint, the innermost side of our lives where the transformation of our whole personhood begins to take place.

God did not intend that mind, emotions and spirit be in conflict or be in competition. God wants our inner lives to be a harmony of thoughts, feelings, and spiritual encounters. But busy heads and turbulent emotions have a way of causing a spiritual blackout. Inner battles for emotional or intellectual supremacy thoroughly distract us from realizing the most precious of our inner treasures, our spirits.

Stillness, quiet, and meditation are the classical methods for sinking deep within ourselves to the stillpoint. The fact that Nicodemus came to Jesus in the stillness of the night favored an invitation to try the exercise of inwardness. Jesus tried a direct approach to open Nicodemus to the absorbing arena of his inner life. That is where Nicodemus would meet the Spirit and permit himself to become the moldable clay. Then he would be born again from above.

Jesus invites us to the same adventure. By the grace of the Sacrament of Baptism we have been born again from above by water and the Holy Spirit. What happened sacramentally, must now be lived existentially. The Spirit is the personal power of the sacrament. But we will not be forced. We must make a free decision to be changed. Even there the Spirit helps us by a gentle love that makes this possible. Our third consideration looks at the easiest way to do this, though for many it proves to be the most difficult.

3. *Love Lifted Me.* The words of an old gospel song fit very well here: "Love lifted me, love lifted me. When I was down and out, love lifted me."

The most quoted line from Christ's dialogue with Nicodemus is the one about God so loving the world that he sent his Son to save us. Those who believe in Jesus will have eternal life. The statement about God's love is what makes the quote so appealing. Here as in so many parts of John's gospel, love and faith are intimately connected. Why so?

When this gospel talks about faith, it is frequently in terms of believing in Jesus, believing in a person. This is faith as an act of relating to a person. This is faith as loving and being loved. Put in another way, this is love expressed through faith. For many people faith is usually associated with believing a doctrine, a divine truth. That is a legitimate understanding of faith. But this must never be separated from faith as a loving union with Jesus.

A loving faith in the person of Jesus will lead to a loving faith in his teachings, doctrines and commands. A loving faith in his personhood will involve a faith in the standards and principles that will govern our behavior. If we concentrate only on the doctrines without an affectionate relation with Jesus, our spiritual life will be dry, harsh, and arid. If we look only at the person of Jesus and pay no attention to his doctrine, then we risk a spirituality that is sentimental, vacuous, and weak.

Nicodemus appeared to be one whose faith was too closely tied to doctrine without a vital and warm relationship to God. Jesus offered him the corrections. His talk about the Spirit — whose essence and behavior is Love — was meant to turn Nicodemus around. His teaching about divine love and salvation crowned his appeal to Nicodemus.

Obviously, this is neither simple nor easy. It embraces the cross. Jesus explained that truth to Nicodemus when he spoke of Moses raising up the bronze serpent in the desert. All who looked on it were healed. Jesus would be lifted up on the cross. Those who looked on him and believed would be saved. Just as love sent Jesus to earth, so love lifts him up both to the cross and to the glory that is revealed by the redemption.

Love lifts us up to our own crosses. Love also lifts us up to experience the revelation of God's glory which is the most authentic response to our desire for happiness. Love as an act of faith must encircle our whole existence. If we bore deeply into our inner world, past the noises of our minds and the turmoil of our emotions, we will find the stillpoint of our spirit. There we discover the ability to receive divine love and to return this love to Jesus, to others, and to our very selves.

The Baptist's Magnificent Spiritual Principle (Jn. 3:22-36)

The ministry of Jesus and his disciples was now active, public and attracting wide attention and praise. In the minds of the disciples of the Baptist, they were being upstaged by this new and dynamic community. The crowds that once streamed to the Jordan had diminished. The person and ministry of their beloved John the Baptist was moving into the shadows. Jesus was now the center of interest. The followers of the Baptist considered this a competitive situation. Their more exciting rival was winning the hearts of people. They complained about this to their spiritual master.

The Baptist replied with his magnificent spiritual principle, "He must increase. I must decrease" (verse 30). He compared himself to the best man at a wedding. The best man does not marry the bride, the bridegroom does. He reminded them that he was not the messiah. The messiah was Jesus, the lamb of God. There is nothing humiliating about this. The honest acknowledgment of another's true greatness is a sign of one's own character and capacity for truthfulness.

The Baptist's magnificent spiritual principle will work very well for us. Jesus must increase. We must decrease. Individually, each of our egos with their sinfulness, pride and self-absorption must decrease. Our identity with love as incarnated by Jesus must increase. Naturally, we fear that losing this aspect of our egos will destroy us. "I fear losing me. I dread the loss of my identity."

But Jesus does not love us to blot us out. He is not a vain master feeding on human egos. Jesus does not inflate himself at our expense. His love recreates our egos — our sense of personhood — with his affection. He makes us new men and women with strong egos informed by grace. Our act of decrease, loss of self, leads to increase, the regaining of self shaped by Christ. We will fear and hate the process. We will exult in the product. This is pure Gospel. Lose the self to gain the self. Decrease in order to increase.

Reflection

1. What experiences have I had where I was ashamed to be seen publicly with another person?
2. Do I place too great an emphasis on credentials and status?
3. In what way can I identify with Nicodemus?
4. If I heard of a saintly person who was performing miracles, what would I think?
5. If someone told me I was in need of deep spiritual change, how would I react?
6. How do I practice the inwardness that leads me to a personal relationship with Jesus?
7. How do I handle my busy head and strong emotions?
8. How could I become the "clay" which Jesus could mold into a "new person"?
9. Why does John's gospel insist on intimately relating faith and love?
10. Why should I decrease so that Jesus might increase? What advantage does that have for my ego?

Prayer

Jesus, you showed great care and concern for Nicodemus. You offered him the vision of change and conversion he needed. You also loved him in a way that led to the beginning of his new faith journey. I come to you with an open heart and ask that you help me decrease so that you will increase. I know that when your influence on my life increases, I will be born again as a new person.

4 The Five Stages of the Samaritan Woman's Conversion

Jesus Dug a Well in Her Awareness (Jn. 4:4-26)

Samaritans and Jews passionately disliked each other. Like so many ethnic hatreds, the source was political and religious. The destructive stream of hostility may be traced back to the civil war that occurred after the death of Solomon. The northern kingdom of Israel fought the southern kingdom of Judea, resulting in a split between the two kingdoms.

When Assyria conquered the north, the Jewish population intermarried with the pagan Assyrians, diluting the faith of the Jews. The capital of the area was Samaria, which in time gave its name to the whole country. The Samaritans accepted only the first five books of the Bible. They did not consider the books of the prophets to be divinely inspired and they rejected the prophetic emphasis on the Jerusalem temple. Samaria was north of Judea and east of the northern district of Galilee.

When Jesus met the Samaritan woman, he did so in a context of tension. There was historical hostility between the two peoples due to the civil war. There was religious hostility between the heretic Samaritans and the true-believing Jews. There was tension between a man and a woman alone by a well, strangers to each other in isolated and dangerous territory.

To feel the human uneasiness between them in modern terms, we need only think of an Israeli male meeting a Palestinian woman in some out-of-the-way desert place. Strangers in the wilderness, heirs to the historical divisions, they were subject to the wariness that any two such individuals might face when meeting one another by chance. We have no way of knowing how much this tension affected them. Whatever initial misgivings there may have been, Jesus calmed the waters and offered the woman the saving love that would transform her.

In our meditation on this scene, we trace five steps in the conversion of the woman. This will include Christ's pastoral approach and her evolving response.

1. Create a Trust Situation (Jn. 4: 7-9). Jesus was tired from his journey and decided to rest by the well while his disciples went into town to purchase food. A woman came to get water. Jesus dispelled the foreseeable tension by asking her for a drink of water. He was non-threatening. He disarmed her by asking her for a favor. He would ask for a favor before giving her a favor. He offered her control of the situation.

He gave her permission to do what she wanted. She could oblige him or refuse him and unburden her hostilities. She chose the latter approach. She asked him how a Jew could ask a Samaritan for a favor. The gospel does not add the details, but imagination might supply the types of remarks she could have added. "You and your people burned our sanctuaries. You use our names as a curse word. You refuse us hospitality. You physically avoid us as though we were lepers. You claim to love God, but despise us."

This is the first step in her conversion. Jesus led her to face her inner loneliness and anxieties. He freed her to express herself to him. She became more objective about herself. He moved her toward a new possibility.

2. Recognize the Other Person's Need — Let That Person Know It (Jn. 4:10-12). Jesus had caught her attention. If she were to understand the gift of God that he was offering her, she would be asking him for the gift. He would satisfy her by giving her living water. Jesus listened to her spiritual longings. He did not reply to her anger. He did not argue with her about cultural prejudices. He saw the shadow that hid her spiritual desires and began the process of sending light into the darkness. In speaking of a gift of God, he touched the universal human eagerness to receive gifts and the deeper human need to receive a divine gift.

His words about living water have two meanings. They refer to running water as contrasted to stagnant pools in desert places. Secondly, they mean waters that satisfy spiritual thirsts. Scripture often used the images of thirst and water when commenting on spiritual needs. "With joy you will draw waters at the fountain of salvation" (Is. 12:3). "As the deer longs for the running streams, so my soul longs for you, my God" (Ps. 42:1). Jesus listened to her spiritual thirst and offered her the living water of God to minister to it. Jesus let her know that he appreciated her inmost longings.

Now he gave her a second permission — to misunderstand what he said. She was not quite ready for self insight. She kept the conversation at an objective level. She stayed at the literal meaning of his words. Getting a little playful and more relaxed, she said he had no bucket. How could he give her any water? Loosening up a little more, she asked him if he thought he were a better man than the patriarch Jacob who built this well. The Old Testament has no record of Jacob building this well or any well for that matter, but a Targum based on Genesis 28:10 says that Jacob did dig a well at Haran. (A Targum was originally an oral interpretation of a biblical passage, then was written down and kept in a collection of such sayings.)

Her anger had subsided. Now she is unwinding a bit more. Her potential for change is growing. She sees something likeable in this supposed enemy. The second step in her conversion is occurring. A Christian conversion. A conversion to the person of Christ. She likes him.

3. Become More Directive (Jn. 4:13-15). Jesus had put her at ease. He had let her control the situation up to this point, but he now took greater charge of their interaction. He observed that a relationship was emerging. They were no longer two strangers at a desert well, but two persons caught up in a process. Just as he had not reacted to her anger in step one, so he did not respond to her nervous literalism in step two.

He continued to minister to her spiritual need. It was clear to him that she wanted a love that was strong, a love that would never betray her. He told her that he could give her something beyond living water. He could offer her everlasting water, a love that would satisfy her forever. Basically, he told her, "I am indeed greater than Jacob who could only give you a well to satisfy physical thirst. I can give you an everlasting water that will quench your spiritual thirst eternally." Intuitively, she knew what he meant.

He let her progress at her own pace. She felt accepted by him. He obviously wanted to give her something of great value. He is not threatening. Nor is he a hostile Jew bent on humiliating her. A sense of wonder began to flow through her whole being. Jesus had awakened in her a basic need. Before she could stop the words, she heard herself saying, "Sir, give me this water."

This was the third stage in her conversion. She wanted the waters of initiation into a community of love. In scriptural and theological language, she yearned for membership in a community of faithful and trustworthy people. This was not explicit in her mind, but it was the substance of her desires.

4. Confront the Person With the Decision to Be Moral (Jn. 4:16-18). Jesus determined that she was now ready for the moment of truth. He knew that her thirst had been undermined by a series of infidelities. Their relationship had evolved to the point where he could speak to her openly. He changed his strategy of non-direction to directive behavior. He said that she should go get her husband. Quickly she said she had no husband. Just as rapidly Jesus replied that she was right. She had five husbands already and the man she lived with now was not her lawful husband.

He asked her to face her immoral choices. There would be no religious conversion so long as the moral issues of her life were not confronted. Only when she was ready to give up her infidelities would she discover true love and experience God. Jesus insisted she consider the possibility of "metanoia" - moral change. Jesus created this crisis event for conversion purposes. He caused an identity crisis in her life. If she emerged from it creatively, she would experience a loss (her old ways of infidelity) and a gain (a new life of trust and love).

As always, Jesus delicately pulled back and let her act freely. She could respond as she chose. He would not coerce faith from her. His shock therapy startled her into calling him a prophet — not just a clairvoyant who mysteriously could read her mind and her past, but a prophet who confronted people with their moral lapses.

She did not want to face that. She dodged the issue. She began to talk about the dispute between Jews and Samaritans as to where authentic worship took place — at Jerusalem or at the Samaritan shrine on Mount Gerizim. He wanted a decision. She wanted a discussion. He thought, "Let's talk about your soul." She replied, "Let's talk theology."

Underneath all of this give and take, the drama of her conversion continued. She cautiously entered the fourth step in the change process — moral conversion.

5. Invite the Person to Faith (Jn. 4:20-26). Jesus accepted her unwillingness to look directly at her moral life. Her discomfort level was too intense. She needed time to let her new awareness work its benefits for her. Jesus did not press her on her divorces and infidelities. He did not act the roaring preacher, intimidating her with accusations, reviling her for her sins, forecasting hellish consequences for her misdeeds. He simply placed a mirror before her soul. She could see well enough what was there. His very presence was enough to keep the mirror steadily before her. His kindness and patience were sufficient to let her absorb this at her own pace. Jesus was more interested in helping her to believe in the future of love than in making her feel miserable about her past.

He went along with her digression into a religious quarrel. He said that the day will come when people will not worship at either Jerusalem or Gerizim, but will adore the Father in Spirit and in truth. The purpose of religious rituals is thus fulfilled when the worshipers permit the ceremonies, songs and readings to open them to the powerful presence of the Spirit working there. This is worshiping in truth. Thereby one is faithful to the goal of liturgy.

Like all digressions, this was buying time to face the real issue at hand. Jesus had dug a well in her awareness and was summoning forth the waters of faith and love. "Whoever drinks the water I will give will never thirst; the water I shall give will become in him a spring of water welling up to eternal life" (verse 14).

Effectively, Jesus is saying: Come. See. Believe. Love.

He waited in the silence of the desert by a well. He had given her the option for love. There is a time in any relationship when the noise of words should stop. The mystery of a person's inner drama deserves reverent reserve. The glory-presence of Jesus was affecting her. A peaceful quiet enveloped her. There was no push from without, only a gathering drive from within.

Slowly, she found herself saying, "I know that the messiah is coming." Out of her own contemplative thoughtfulness, she spoke from her heart, which is ready to meet that savior. She did want the everlasting water after all. Her inner drive to faith and love has uttered its plea for salvation.

Jesus simply replied, "I am he, the one who is speaking with you." He gave her the love she sought. The expression "I am," which will appear so frequently in John, echoed the word of God to Moses at the burning bush. When Moses wanted to know God's name, God said, "I am." Jesus is God in the flesh. He confided in this woman his most precious secret, "I am." At that moment she came to faith.

This describes the fifth stage in her conversion, her total, personal commitment to Christ, to community, to morality, and to evangelical witness. This last aspect of her conversion is illustrated by her leaving her water pot at the well, going back to her town and preaching the Good News to her relatives, friends and acquaintances.

Behold the Convert Who
Becomes an Evangelist (Jn. 4:27-42)

Jesus amazed her with his insights into her heart. She could have used a psalm verse to explain his power. "You understand my thoughts from afar. . . . Even before a word is on my tongue, behold, O Lord, you know the whole of it" (Ps. 139:1ff). Jesus saw the sleeping person inside her heart. Like a surgeon who sees a disease, but who sees the health that follows when the sickness is cut away, Jesus compassionately turned her away from a disappointing life into one full of meaning.

The apostles returned with the food supplies and set out a meal, but Jesus touched nothing. They urged him to eat. Jesus was still too absorbed in the contemplative moment of the woman's conversion. He had revealed his glory and the woman had received the grace of loving faith. The experience had intensified his evangelical appetite. "I have food to eat of which you do not know" (verse 32).

When he was ready to talk, he reminded his disciples of the amber fields of grain which they had seen on their northward journey. Those fields were ripe for the harvest. He used the agricultural image to illustrate an evangelization message. Many people were ready for salvation, but there must be evangelists willing and able to bring them the possibility. In Matthew 9:37-8, Jesus said, "The harvest is abundant but the laborers are few; so ask the master of the harvest to send out laborers for his harvest." The evangelizers must remember they are engaged in a divine work. Even the call to evangelize was a work of the Spirit.

This whole section closed like a Greek play with a chorus of Samaritans, the leading lady, the apostles, and Jesus all gathered front and center stage. The Samaritans reported their conversion to Jesus through the preaching of the Woman at the Well. They urged Jesus to stay with them so he could increase their faith and convert those yet to be brought into his community of disciples. The conclusion was like the stirring end of a magnificent drama. They all turn to Jesus and acclaim him: We know that you are really the Savior of the world (see verse 42).

A Model For Evangelization

This conversion narrative is a superb example of person-to-person evangelization. The five steps that Jesus followed are wisdom tactics for all evangelizers. While this is not the only way to do it, it is one that has been modeled for us by the Son of God become flesh. We can adapt it to our situations. We are not likely to improve on it. This is full Gospel evangelizing because the woman is not only converted, but she becomes an evangelizer herself. Jesus has not only given each of us the call to evangelize in our baptism, he also has shown us a sensitive and compassionate method for doing it.

The Cure of the Nobleman's Son (Jn. 4:46-54)

Jesus loved Galilee.

After all, there is no place like home.

Jesus returned to Cana in Galilee where he had performed the wine miracle, the first sign and revelation of his glory presence among us. A royal official from Capernaum heard he was there and came to ask him to heal his son who was dying. Just as when his mother had asked him to help the wedding couple, Jesus at first resisted performing a miracle. He decried the fact that unless people saw signs and wonders, they would not believe.

Jesus meant that the astonishment a miracle engendered often captivated people's curiosity and satisfied their taste for the sensational and the startling. But it did not necessarily lead them to faith in him. God made the same point to Moses, "Despite the many signs and wonders I will work in the land of Egypt, the pharaoh will not listen to you" (Ex. 7:3-4).

The nobleman persisted in his prayer to Jesus, "Sir, come down before my child dies" (verse 49). Jesus assured him his son would live. Later that day, the nobleman set out for home. His twenty mile, overnight journey took him across the Galilean hills and down the road to Capernaum. Servants met him before he arrived home. They told him the joyful news that his son was healed. It happened at 1 p.m. the previous day — just when Jesus told him his son would be all right.

This was the second sign whereby Jesus revealed his glory presence. John writes, "[The nobleman] and his whole household came to believe" (verse 53). The purpose of the sign-miracles of Jesus was to call people to faith in him. In the first sign at Cana, Christ's disciples began to have faith in him. In the second sign at Cana, a nobleman's family also came to believe in him. Miracles do not always solicit faith. If people stop at the thrill a miracle causes they will simply regard it as they would a dog dancing or an acrobat balancing a glass of water on his head. If they probe further and obtain a hint of the glory-presence of Jesus reaching them through the miracle, they will be prompted to faith.

Reflection

1. How do I share my faith with other believers? How have I shared my faith with unbelievers?
2. Why is trust important in helping people convert to Jesus?
3. What is the value of permitting people to come to Christ at their own pace, but with help from us?
4. How does moral conversion fit in the process of conversion?
5. If I needed to confront someone about a moral issue in a conversion process, how might I do it?
6. Why should I be patient when a prospective convert sometimes dodges an essential matter?
7. This chapter describes Jesus as reaching a point where he remains present — but silent — in his evangelizing of the Samaritan woman. Why would he do that?
8. Do I know any converts? Do I know their conversion stories? Do they try to bring others to conversion?
9. What have I learned from Christ's pastoral approach in evangelizing the Samaritan woman?
10. How would I react if I actually witnessed a miracle?

Prayer

Evangelizing Jesus, you have called me to share my faith with believer and unbeliever alike. In my baptism you uttered that call. I confess that I have to pay more attention to this aspect of my Christian calling. Your Gospel example of loving, patient but insistent evangelizing is an inspiring example for me. Motivate me to become what I have been called to be — an evangelizing person.

5 A Miracle at the House of Mercy

Jesus Visits Bethesda (Jn. 5:1-19)

Jesus returned to Jerusalem for a religious festival. Jews were expected to go to Jerusalem for the three greatest feasts: Passover, Pentecost, and Tabernacles. Very likely, this was the Jewish feast of Pentecost, which occurred fifty days after Passover and celebrated the giving of the covenant at Sinai.

Jesus entered the city by the Sheep Gate, through which sheep were brought to the temple for sacrifice. He visited a miracle shrine, Bethesda, the House of Mercy. It was situated near the Sheep Gate. He saw the centerpiece of the shrine, a pool where healing miracles periodically occurred. One tradition stated that an angel came from time to time and stirred the waters. The first one into the pool after that would be cured. In any event, miracles occurred after intermittent bubblings of the waters. Around the pool were five porches where the sick, blind, and crippled would wait for a possible healing.

Archaeologists have discovered this pool, just as described in John, near St. Anne's Church. It is 220-feet wide and 315-feet long. Colonnades on all sides frame the porches. Stairways at the corners facilitated entrance into the waters. Springs were the probable sources of the waters. Changes in water pressure could cause the "stirring or bubbling effect" noted by the gospel.

Jesus met a man there who told him his sad story. He had been ill for thirty-eight years. Painfully, he had made his way to the House of Mercy many times but never obtained a cure. Jesus asked him if he would like to be healed. He told Jesus he had no friend to help him get into the pool after the stirring of the waters. He was too slow to get in on time. Jesus told him to arise, pick up his mat and walk. The poor man felt charged with amazing new energy. Joyously he stood up and walked.

This lovely incident carries forward the theme of water in John's gospel. The Baptist had preached that Jesus would baptize with water and the Spirit. Jesus had told Nicodemus that he needed the profound personal change that would be caused by rebirth in water and the Spirit.

The water for washing the body at Cana was changed into wine, forecasting the Eucharistic Blood of Jesus which would cleanse our souls from the tyranny of sins. The conversion of the Samaritan woman occurred when the waters of grace warmed her heart. Now, by a pool famed for its healing qualities, Jesus cured this man.

In healing this man's body, Jesus showed he was interested in total person, soul and body. He restored the soul of a woman by a well. He rejuvenated the body of a man by a pool. By connecting his acts with water imagery, Jesus took the simplest of elements and showed he stood for human life in its bodily and spiritual forms.

Water is absolutely necessary for life. Today we are more aware of this when we see environmental threats from chemical wastes. We worry about lead in the water that causes disease to our bodies, and acid rain that kills trees and plants. We demand living water that is healthy for our physical well being, not killing water that would harm us. In the desert culture where Jesus ministered, pure water was a valued gift. Jesus took this central fact of life and used it to illustrate the truth that his "water" of love and grace was absolutely necessary for spiritual life, which gives purpose and meaning to our bodily life.

Ultimately, only God can be the author of life. An incident linked to the cure at the House of Mercy taught that Jesus was the divine source of life. The healing occurred on the sabbath. The religious leaders heard of this, found the man and told him he should not be carrying his mat because that was "working" on the sabbath. He replied that the man who cured him told him to take up his mat and walk. They wanted to know the healer's identity, but the cured man had no idea who it was.

Sometime later, Jesus found the man at the temple, identified himself and told the man to sin no more. The man went to the religious leaders and let them know it was Jesus who cured him. They approached Jesus and criticized him for his behavior. In similar situations in the synoptic gospels,[*] Jesus argued on humanitarian grounds that this was the compassionate thing to do. Here he used a

---

[*]"There is an impressive agreement — verbal and sequential — among the first three gospels: Matthew, Mark and Luke. For purposes of comparison, these gospels can be put into parallel columns. This ordering of materials is known as a 'synopsis.' As a result, Matthew, Mark and Luke have come to be known as the Synoptic Gospels." — Peter Stravinskas, ed., *Our Sunday Visitor's Catholic Encyclopedia* (Huntington, IN: Our Sunday Visitor, 1991).

divine argument, "My Father is at work until now, so I am at work" (verse 17). The miracle demonstrated his equality with God.

The leaders saw his point. Genesis taught that God worked six days and rested on the seventh, or sabbath. But that meant God had finished the works of creation. God obviously still had to "work" because he was sustaining the world by his providential care. That is what Jesus meant when he said that "My Father is working until now." By adding, "So I am at work," he identified himself with God. He does what God does. This was blasphemy to the ears of the religious leaders, an act deserving of death. The text says they made plans for his death, for he made himself equal to God.

Jesus Strives to Awaken Spiritual Awareness (Jn. 5:19-30)

We all live at the edge of mystery and ignore it. We do not surrender to the stillness that would open us to God. We turn our inner light away from God. We build a screen between ourselves and God, each day putting more shadows on it until the darkness is so great we cannot believe God can be present to us. We plunge our energies into surviving and cease to appreciate the life we have preserved. We let ambition consume us and then lament what it produces for us.

Jesus saw this problem in the faces of the religious leaders. They were the ministers of the mystery of God, yet they failed to sense the divine warmth when it came to them in the person of Jesus. What blocked their awareness? In general, we can say they were too involved in themselves to see God visiting them in Jesus.

Their sense of self was tied up with controlling the way God can be experienced. They were in the business of making people be submissive to them in religious matters. They sought their pleasure in the sheer mastery of others. They forgot that the rituals, beliefs and ceremonies of religion, committed to their care, were like pure windows that could reveal divine Love inviting people to receive affection and forgiveness.

Jesus did not treat them with hostility or disdain. He strove to loosen them from their self imprisonment, their attachment to a self that enjoys controlling religious mystery. To help them see, Jesus took a simple example of a young man apprenticing to his father, much as he himself did in the carpenter shop of his father Joseph.

The novice is expected to learn by looking at what his father does.

The wisdom of the carpenter is passed onto the son who observes carefully how to cut, sand, shape, varnish, paint, and respect the grain of the wood. When the son takes his turn at the bench, the father watches to see that the apprentice does what he has seen. Mere observation becomes personal experience. In time, the gifts of the son cause him to bring his own creativity to the task, but only after carefully imitating the process he witnessed from his father. As the son matures both in the skill and a creativity unique to him, the father smiles. Father and son have become one in a mutual goal.

Jesus drew his listeners to see that his relationship with his heavenly Father was something like that, only more intimate and effective. A carpenter will simply evoke a chair or a table from a piece of wood. But God the Father does a lot more. The Father gives life. So does the Son. Gently Jesus tried to make them see that the gift of living health he imparted to the sick man at the House of Mercy was but a glimpse of the abundant divine life he could give them. He and the Father can share this life, this Love, with them.

Jesus appealed to their own hunger for absolute love. He tried to shake them loose from their attachment to public status. He reached into their inner lives and asked them to wake up to real affection and true religion. They were missing out on the true joy of living. They settled for less, for a cheap substitute, the small, passing pleasure of people's grudging submission to their authority.

He gave them the opportunity of a lifetime, a personal meeting with God, as physical and historical as human presence can get. This was not a dry theology lesson, but a personal encounter, an experience of how Father and Son are so willing to love and be life giving.

Sadly, he observed their resistance, their unwillingness to let go of the selves so invested in religious control. They preferred the false self to the true one that could be on fire with desire to love and be loved magnificently. Jesus offered them the champagne of living water. They chose the stagnant water of their own prejudices.

This led to Christ's words about judgement. "(The Father) has given all judgment to his Son" (verse 22). His listeners have been given the choice to find their real selves and thus begin a dialogue with God. Jesus respected their freedom. They were at liberty to get in touch with Love, or to refuse. They may continue with a life of pretense, or they could become real persons. Their choice brought consequences.

Every cause has an effect. If they lied to themselves, they will never find out the truth about their destiny. The glory-presence of Jesus waited there, sending forth waves of light and love. Jesus was a judge, but they will cause their own judgment by their choices. Jesus had attempted to plant in their awarenesses the seeds of their true identity, their authentic reality, their only real hope for happiness and love. He has provided a force field of grace where this could happen.

Jesus' listeners had a chance to pass from death to life. As they pondered the daring challenge he had given them, they heard him raise the issue of death. The day will come when the dead will hear the voice of the Son of God and rise to life. Those who emerge from the tombs with a record of love will have a resurrection unto life. Those who rise with a history of sin, will be condemned. Hence they must consider the eternal consequences of the challenge presented to them. Jesus is not just persuading them to seek temporary happiness, but everlasting joy.

The Burning Lamp and the Listener's Unbelief (Jn. 5:31-47)

Next, Jesus appealed to their very human need to trust his credibility. If he did not seem believable, perhaps they could be convinced by others who testified on his behalf. They had admired John the Baptist. Many of them had journeyed to the Jordan, confessed their sins and been washed in the Jordan waters. It is possible they desired to believe in Jesus. What is clear from the gospel is that Jesus desired their faith even more powerfully.

Whether they liked it or not, they heard from the Baptist a ringing act of faith in Jesus. The Baptist was like a burning and shining lamp who awoke long dormant depths of faith in his listeners. Jesus invoked John's testimony on his behalf. If the Baptist believed in him, could they not open themselves to this possibility? Jesus went further and asked them to look attentively at the signs of glory he had performed. Through these miracles, the Father testified to the Son's truth. Thus Jesus presented them with evidence from the greatest prophet of the day, and the greatest of all witnesses — God.

Jesus could see that even such powerful witnesses did not affect them. They knew so well the words of Scripture. But they failed to perceive the Living Word in front of them. They settled for a text and missed a person. The words of Scripture fell off their lips like dead leaves in autumn. The words should have risen like eagles from their hearts to meet God. Regrettably, this did not happen.

They loved the praise from the people, the praise that stroked their egos. They loved themselves too much to bother about loving God. Self absorption caused their failure to believe. This process makes the self God. But what is there about a self that it should become an idol? The self loses out when made into a mere idol. Such attachment to self is foolishness. Only attachment to the non-self, meaning a focus on God brings about genuine self realization. Seeking praise of self obtains mere flattery and shrinks the person. When the self praises God, the heart expands and the person grows.

Glorifying self is an attitude that kills faith. "How can you believe when you accept praise from one another and do not seek the praise that is from God?" (verse 44). Jesus had tried to be patient and gentle with them, but they were so closed to him that he decided to adopt the forthright, fiery confrontation typical of a prophet. Even this approach might have its conversion potential. Strong language has often affected the human heart.

In any case, his words were also directed at innocent bystanders. He wanted them to know what blind guides they followed. He especially caught everyone's attention when he said that the one who will forcefully accuse them of their lack of faith was Moses, who foresaw that people would reject the offer of salvation in messianic times. None of this worked as we will see in the story of the Passion. The defenders of the faith will kill the author of faith. The would-be proclaimers of salvation will crucify the savior.

Reflection

1. What does Bethesda mean?
2. What Catholic miracle shrine is centered around water?
3. How has the theme of water been used in the gospel up to this point?
4. Why has water in our time become such an issue with the environ mentalists?
5. Why would Jesus have tried to evangelize the religious leaders?
6. What are the reasons for the resistance of the religious leaders to having faith in Jesus?

7. In what ways do I screen out God's presence from my awareness?
8. Share some stories about people whose self absorption causes them to lack faith in Jesus?
9. Why did Jesus speak so strongly against the religious leaders?
10. How could the religious leaders be such students of the Word of God in Scripture, yet fail to recognize the Word of God when they met him?

Prayer

Jesus, giver of the "water" of grace and love, look at the thirst in my soul and fill me with the waters of salvation. Call forth from my heart the desire for you and meet that desire with your love. Help me to know myself in order to turn my inner life always toward you. Show me how to put some love in my life and some life in my love.

6 Amazing Bread, How Sweet the Taste

The Bread Miracle in the Desert (Jn. 6:1-15)

It was springtime.

The Passover feast would soon begin.

The flowers appeared in the land and the sumptuous velvet grasses carpeted the hills.

Jesus and his apostles sailed across the waters of Galilee to its western shore. They aimed for a quiet area where they could enjoy some solitude and ponder the mystery of spring and the wonder of God.

A multitude of people had arrived in Capernaum, coming to hear the hope-filled words of Jesus and bringing their sick to be touched by his healing hand. They discovered that Jesus had just departed for the western shore, and they could see his boat heading for the small fishing port at Bethsaida Julias, just opposite Capernaum. The lake of Galilee is relatively narrow at this northern end. This meant that if the people walked briskly enough around the lake they could be at the other side not long after Jesus arrived.

From his boat Jesus could see the long procession of people, marching in hope, singing the psalms of desire for God. The hunger in their hearts for the bread of God pressed them to journey to Jesus. The shadows in their inner lives urged them to walk toward the light. Jesus watched that stream of humanity determined to find him and willing to walk many miles to be in his presence. Their tender faith transformed them into pilgrims. Jesus felt great compassion for them for he saw how much care they needed. They were sheep without a shepherd. An inner spiritual drive pushed them to experience his presence. They needed spiritual food. Jesus would not disappoint them.

The majestic line of 5,000 pilgrims met Jesus at the western shore. Like a good shepherd he led them up the nearby mountain where he sat down and spoke to them of hope, forgiveness, and salvation. Some have wondered how he could be heard by everyone in a throng like this. In ancient times, a system of heralds, or "loud speakers," made this possible. Placed strategically throughout the crowd, the heralds relayed the message to the vast assembly.

In this situation, Christ's speaking style would be relaxed, leisurely, unhurried. He would paint a word picture, an aphorism or a wisdom saying in a condensed, powerful sentence. Like wind brushing over a field of grain, his word was carried by the heralds to his listeners. Flowing back to him from this vast assembly was a murmur of assent and an audible praise of God. This was a dialogue of faith. St. Matthew described a similar situation in his record of the Sermon on the Mount and Luke did the same in his memoir of the Sermon in the Valley. John does not report the words of Christ's communion with his beloved people in this mountain scene. He will wait until after the bread miracle to chronicle in splendid cadences the Bread of Life dialogue at the site of the Capernaum synagogue.

Only imagination can supply what Jesus probably said here. We will go no further than to suggest that he meditated with his spiritually hungry audience on the glory of the forthcoming Passover. This would include a reflection on the gracious acts of God that led their ancestors to freedom across the Red Sea and to a love bond with the Lord at Sinai after a pilgrimage across the desert. He would have applied that message to their present situation and proclaimed the first truths about the new Passover to be created by him.

There was no Passover without a meal. He asked Philip where food could be found for so great a crowd. Philip shrugged and said that even a year's worth of salary would not buy enough food to feed a group like this. Andrew pointed to a boy who had five barley loaves and two fish. What good would that be for this throng?

Jesus ordered the people to sit down on the lush spring grass. He took the loaves, blessed them and distributed them to the people. He did the same with the fish. His bread miracle fed everyone. There was enough left over to fill twelve baskets. He had fed their souls with his nourishing word. Then he hosted a kind of outdoor "Passover Meal," a divine picnic, in which he ministered to the physical hunger of his people. He witnessed his concern for the total well being of all these men, women, and children.

Jesus' bread miracle in the wilderness matched his wine miracle at Cana. Taken together they formed the core symbolism of the Eucharist, of which he would speak in his Bread of Life dialogue. It is no mistake that he treated the bread with steps associated with Eucharistic ritual. His "taking, blessing, breaking and giving" the bread modeled what would be done in the first Christian Eucharists and in our own today. In the synoptic gospels the Lord's Supper, takes place in an Upper Room. In John's gospel, the prefigurement of the Lord's Supper takes place on a mountain at Passover time.

Christ's words thrilled the hearts of his listeners. His Bread Miracle unintentionally fired their practical need for a political messiah. In the ecstasy of that mellow evening on a green mountainside, they surged forward with the intention of lifting him up on their shoulders and carrying him back to Capernaum as their messianic king. They shouted "Prophet," meaning messiah. They missed the point of his ministry that afternoon. Jesus had no intention of fulfilling their false expectations. He mysteriously disappeared and went to a place of solitude on the mountain.

Jesus Walks Across the Water (Jn. 6:16-24)

That evening the apostles boarded the boat and sailed back to Capernaum. Jesus stayed on the mountain for a night of prayer. After the apostles were a few miles out to sea, darkness fell. Angry clouds and winds brought a sudden and dangerous storm. Though they were used to the sea as fishermen, and despite the fact they had weathered many storms, they always feared catastrophe when put at the mercy of the sea.

They had sailing skills for maneuvering and courage to forge ahead, but they were all too aware of the frail hold their little boat had when faced with the unpredictable push of the winds and the threat of being swamped in the waves. The synoptic accounts of this storm at sea clearly point out the panic of the apostles in the face of this life-threatening situation.

Thus the apostles found themselves in an extreme crisis. They faced the possibility of death by drowning. Intense and palpable fear gripped them. It has been said that nothing concentrates the mind more than facing the barrel of a gun in the hand of a murderer. The fact of dying by drowning just as surely focused the minds of the apostles. The basic need for survival blocked out all other thoughts, but also released fundamental, inner religious attitudes.

In the Second World War the chaplains noted there were "no atheists in foxholes." The threat of death quickens one's thoughts of God. Even the hardiest secularist will suddenly say, "Lord, save me!" Or burst out with, "O God!" Which is exactly what the apostles did say in the synoptic versions of this story. Potential shipwreck experiences have a way of stirring up dormant faith.

In John's account there is no reference to the calming of the waters, nor is there a description of apostles terrorized by the storm. That part of the story is assumed. John knew that his readers and listeners would be familiar with a narrative as vivid as this one. So he moved immediately to the faith experience which is found in all the reports. John did note the fear of the apostles, but it was not of the storm. Instead they were frightened by the vision of Jesus walking toward them across the waters.

On the one hand they had the childish fear of seeing a ghost. On the other hand they experienced awe, a tremendous sense of fearful wonder in beholding the divine majesty of Jesus mastering the water, doing what only God could do. The storm at sea had become an occasion for a revelation of the glory of Jesus. The apostles experienced his divine presence. Jesus confirmed the revelation with his words, Do not be afraid. I AM (see verse 30). The "I am" is a form of the divine name received by Moses at the scene of the Burning Bush. In John's gospel, Jesus will often use the "I am" statements, unmistakable references to the Word of God become flesh.

In the roaring of the waters, in the midst of death, in the life-threatening crisis, Jesus revealed his glory and saving love. He begged them to let go of their fear and invited them to a faith commitment to him. As God the Father had led the people of Israel safely through the raging waters of the Red Sea, so now God the Son escorted the apostles safely through the storm waters of Lake Galilee. "They wanted to take him into the boat, but the boat immediately arrived at the shore to which they were heading" (verse 21).

John's description is resolutely supernatural. His view of the miracle is not the calming of the waters, so much as a wondrous transfer of the alarmed apostles to the safety of the shore, like a repeat performance of the Passover delivery of Israel at the Red Sea. Still, his attention is less on a miracle than on the revelation of the glory of Jesus and his call of the apostles to faith. If in any way they shared the mistaken notion of messiah proclaimed at the bread miracle, they should be disabused of that idea in this event. Jesus is not a mere earthly king, but the Lord who has come to love them into salvation from death and sin.

The Dialogue on the Amazing Bread (Jn. 6:22-71)

The scene shifts to Capernaum, a northern town near the place where the Jordan flows into Galilee lake. This prosperous community owned the Seven Wells whose plentiful waters, conveyed by an aqueduct, were used to irrigate the nearby plain and drive pottery and tanning mills. They fed a cistern which provided water for an elegant, mosaic-inlaid Roman bath. Today we can find ruins there of an ornate second century synagogue, built on the ruins of a simpler one that dated from Christ's time.

Throughout the centuries, Christians have collected ancient millstones, used for grinding wheat and barley flour, and brought them to Capernaum and placed them around this synagogue. Those solid old millstones stir up pictures of wheat harvests, the feel of fresh flour, the smell of bread baking, the hearty satisfaction of a meal of bread and lamb and salad and wine. For the modern pilgrim they evoke the memory of the dialogue on the Bread of Life which could very well have taken place in the assembly area outside the synagogue.

A Passover Process

Jesus proceeded to take his listeners through what might be called a "Passover Process." This means he offered them the opportunity to pass over their old ways of living, feeling and thinking to a new approach. His process consisted of four steps. (1). Let go of false views of religion. (2). Become involved with the person of Jesus. (3). Prepare to be broken and given. (4). Surrender to the person of Jesus.

1. Let Go of False Views of Religion (Jn. 6:22-34). Jesus' bread miracle had captivated them. They failed to make him a king, but they could not resist being near him and raising him to the status of a religious celebrity. They surged into the assembly area by the Capernaum synagogue, where they continued to project their false expectations on him. Jesus had subdued their political passions for the moment. Now he must disengage them from making him a cult figure, a kind of one-man, spiritual welfare agency.

His warm sermon made them feel good. His bread miracle unintentionally generated a false dependency on him. For them he was not really a person with whom they could get involved, so much as a mood satisfier and a stomach filler. They were consumers of religious emotion and wonder bread. They had an agenda based on self satisfaction. Jesus had a mission founded on a challenging personal relationship with them.

He quietly led them into the first stage of a liberating Passover process. Jesus began by getting them to talk about their reactions to him. Why were they so enthusiastically seeking him? What did they think of the experiences of the loaves and fishes? They said that not since Moses had fed their ancestors with manna had anyone nourished them so marvelously. Jesus proceeded to help them see the limitations of bread satisfaction. Bread and fish take care of a basic need. But what do you do after you eat? What happens between meals? Are there not other needs to be met? What about financial, cultural and spiritual needs? What about love that never fails?

They all knew that the bread from their bakeries bore the seal of the baker. Perhaps Jesus held up a loaf of bread for them to inspect. A visual aid to fix their attention. He might have pointed to the seal and commented that this loaf came from Josiah the baker. The seal identified the baker and stood for quality bread. Jesus applied this visual aid to the desert manna. God was the real "baker" of that bread. Moses was simply the delivery man.

Carefully, Jesus led them to see that the bread he had given them on the mountain was like the manna. It offered only temporary satisfaction. He could give them "God Bread" that would satisfy their need for a love that never fails. When love is the issue, the seal of God the "baker" will be found.

Jesus touched their basic needs. They were charmed by the idea of a bread that would keep them from ever being hungry again. They were warmed by the feeling that their desire for boundless affection could actually be met.

In their minds, they mixed up miracle bread and the love offering, and they were not yet aware of the faith challenge and personal sacrifice that would be asked of them. Innocently, but avidly, they urged Jesus to give them this new kind of bread-love.

They took the first tentative step in the Passover Process.

2. Become Involved With the Person of Jesus (Jn. 6:35-50).
Then Jesus brought the whole discussion to the personal level. He told them that the bread image should lead them to think of a person. Not just any person, but God. "I AM the bread of life.... I came down from heaven" (verses 35, 38). These were overpowering words for them, filled with mystery. They felt disoriented. They saw a human being. They knew of his modest reputation as a competent carpenter. Yet in some startling way he had become an inspiring preacher and a remarkable healer.

He had resisted their attempt to make him a political leader. They could accept that. The risks were high. And he still had a mother to look after. But now he had raised new issues they never dreamed of. He was applying the "I AM" to himself. He was the Son of God the Father and came to do the Father's will. He spoke of personal intimacy with God. The extraordinary revelation subdued them momentarily. They became profoundly reflective. Cool breezes came from Galilee. The late afternoon sun warmed the toast colored stones of the synagogue. A lone eagle floated in the sky. Silence gripped them.

What should they make of his claims? Had he let his fame go to his head? Prophets had talked about personal intimacy with God, but they always kept the distinction between God and themselves. Their own present experience of religion was mostly doing the rituals, saying prayers, trying to live good moral lives and tying feasts to cultural celebrations.

Jesus understood their inability to grasp and accept the mystery he had revealed to them. He did not proceed to explain the mystery, but rather intensified his personal appeal to them. He had shown himself to be a caring person, nourishing their spirits and bodies. He invited them to friendship with him, a relationship based on trust. He asked them to believe in him. If they can believe in his love, they will be able to appreciate his mystery and come to understand his truth.

Love can penetrate the darkness of mystery. Love has an inner light that enables the lover to accept and comprehend divine truth. By reaching into their hearts to form a love bond with him, Jesus hoped to initiate them into believing in his mystery and truth. To be involved with him as a person meant they had to shed the very self interest that had attracted them to him. He was asking them to love him and accept his love.

But they wanted to use him, not love him. Absorbed in consuming his sermons and miracle bread, they could only think of exploiting him, not loving him. Nonetheless, Jesus held them by his presence and he tried to bring them to a third stage of the Passover Process — the most difficult phase of all.

3. Prepare to be Broken and Given (Jn. 6:51-58). Jesus never believed in hiding the truth from people. Nor was he shy about appealing to people's capacity for heroism. He knew how great was the potential for human courage, and he understood the secret thrill every person feels when challenged to be brave and sacrificial. He was also aware of how scared those same people will feel when confronted with the decision to act on a command to live up to a high ideal. He had moved inside the Capernaum Synagogue for this part of the discourse. Underneath that waning afternoon sun, which shed a mellow glow within that room, Jesus stirred up exactly those conflicting emotions of courage and glory, of fear and flight.

He used the magnificent language of Eucharist to elevate them to a level of mystery and a level of choice they had never known before. Even as he honored their deepest drive to be noble, he risked surfacing their embarrassing wish to be weak and evasive.

Scholars have often pointed out that John's gospel has no narrative of the Words of Institution of the Eucharist. Instead, John's teaching about Christ's institution of the Eucharist occurred here in the Bread of Life discourse. What made its presence here so exalting and spiritually compelling was its integration into a profound communion between him and the congregation in "Synagogue Square" at Capernaum on a splendid afternoon by the refreshing waters of Galilee. What grips the reader is the extraordinary and forthright supernatural probing Jesus undertakes in order to awaken the deepest layer of their capacity for mystery and courage.

This is the context for hearing his words, otherwise so alien to the community at Capernaum. "Whoever eats my flesh and drinks my blood has eternal life, and I will raise him on the last day. For my flesh is true food, and my blood is true drink" (verses 54-55). The wine miracle at Cana and the bread miracle on the mountain were symbolic preparations for this teaching of Jesus. He spoke unequivocally now. The bread *is* body. The wine *is* his blood. Divine life is received when we eat his body and drink his blood.

Today it is popular to thin out the mysteries of Jesus. The assumption is that modern people are either too sophisticated to believe such truths, or else too weak to absorb such mighty realities. Some have argued that even Jesus never laid so much divine truth on his listeners during his lifetime. Instead these were teachings given later in the early church and simply reconstructed by John to have occurred in Christ's earthly ministry. The assumption is that Jesus was astute enough to know such truths would have been too much for his listeners without extensive preparation.

But most people, both now and then, are much stronger than we give them credit for. Moreover, the human spirit is far more receptive to divine reality than the advocates of hesitancy contend. God made the human spirit to thirst for God. Jesus honored that Capernaum congregation with revelations about his divinity and the Eucharist. He was not afraid of "spiritual overload." He had a great respect for the capabilities of the human spirit.

Besides, there had been remote and proximate preparation for his revelations. The history of salvation, the visions of the prophets and the cumulative faith of over a thousand years of communion with the God of the covenant were the remote preparation. His own ministry of word and sign, as well as of personal outreach, was the proximate preparation. God's people were accustomed to divine revelation. They may have resisted it, or not lived by it, but they were culturally and spiritually equipped for it.

As if the revelations were not enough, Jesus pointed out that he would be broken (his body to be eaten — his blood to be drunk) and given "for the life of the world." His doctrinal teaching was essentially tied to a moral challenge. The Eucharist and the passion go together. Eucharistic living involves sacrificial love. His followers would also have to be willing to be broken and given so that love and salvation will be available to the world. Jesus had not spared them the strenuous demands of the third stage of the Passover Process.

4. Surrender to the Person of Jesus (Jn. 6:60-71). In John's gospel there is frequent reference to the glory-presence of Jesus. We all know people who have the gift of personal presence. When they enter a room, they "fill" it. Jesus possessed this charisma, not in the sense of bowling people over, but by projecting a warm intensity, an attractive affection that drew people to him. Quite possibly his glory-presence never burned with more warm-heartedness than at this moment in his revelation about the Eucharist.

He thirsted and yearned for their personal surrender to him because of the magnificent benefits his splendid love offering would produce for them. He did not argue or try to force them. He rested in silence and awaited their response. Many decided that his invitation and challenge was too hard for them. They could not accept it. Some of them were shocked by what he demanded of them. Jesus commented that only a faith surrender would reveal the meaning of the mystery for them.

Jesus had risked losing disciples that day. Many of them left him. He turned to the twelve. "Do you also want to leave?" Simon Peter answered, "Master, to whom shall we go? You have the words of eternal life. We have come to believe and are convinced that you are the Holy One of God" (verses 67-69). This is a rich variation of Peter's confession of faith at Caesarea Philippi (Mt. 16:16). Peter's faith here embraces the Eucharist as well as the divinity and messiahship of Jesus. With the grace of the resurrection and the coming of the Spirit, Peter will begin to appreciate what he is saying at Capernaum. The seed of faith that day will flower after Easter.

In the Last Supper accounts in the synoptic gospels, Jesus began by referring to one who would betray him. In this Eucharistic Passover Process, Jesus also speaks of a betrayer. "Is not one of you a devil?" (verse 70). So ends this powerful discourse on the Bread of Life. Amazing Bread, how sweet the taste! Jesus carefully spelled out his revelation in personal terms. He asked for belief and surrender to him. Some believed and some did not. That will mark the whole history of Christianity from Capernaum to this present hour — even to the last moment of history.

Reflection

1. If I had been among those present at the bread miracle, how might I have reacted?
2. When I am in my own storm at sea — my troubles, anxieties, tragedies — how do I welcome Jesus to my situation?
3. In what way do I approach religion as a spiritual consumer of

bread and emotional stroking? What do I think of that?

4. How can doctrinal teaching help me appreciate Jesus as a person?
5. Why was Jesus not afraid to reveal so much mystery (his divinity and the Eucharist) to the Capernaum community?
6. What is there about my inner spirit that makes it possible to receive such wondrous revelations?
7. How do I connect the Bread of Life with Jesus as person?
8. How much do I resist being "broken and given" as part of my Eucharistic calling?
9. What has helped me to surrender to Jesus in faith?
10. How do I help others believe in Jesus?

Prayer

Bread of Life, Wine of Salvation, Jesus I adore you, love you, surrender myself to you. I believe. Help my unbelief. Stretch my inner spirit to receive an even greater fullness of your mystery and love. Fill me with the love that opens me to mystery. Put power in my faith so I will not be afraid to give myself to you. Teach me to see that being "broken and given" actually heals me and others.

7   Thirsty Ones! Come to the Water!

Farmers love good harvests. They also love water, especially when they happen to live in desert climates. Agricultural festivals centered on harvests and rain are as old as history itself. The genius of Judaism — which Christianity would also evidence — was taking such nature feasts and making them religious festivals as well.

The feast of Tabernacles celebrated the autumn harvest and the hope for winter rain to help along the spring growing period. It also honored the memory of Israel's forty year pilgrimage in the desert after the Red Sea Crossing. As the farmers engaged in rain making rituals, the priest carried a golden bowl of water from the pool of Siloam to the temple where he poured it on the altar. The priest prayed for rain, but also implored God for an outpouring of the divine spirit of compassion. Rain for the earth. A divine spirit for the human heart.

There was a playful quality about this feast. Families built tents made out of branches and leaves and camped out for the eight days of the feast. This recalled the "tent days" of their ancestors in the desert. They looked back with nostalgia on the simplicity of life and religion in those olden times. In those nomadic days, people carried the ark of God (also called the ark of the Covenant) with them, and felt like free spirits in their never ending journey.

Their faith seemed more dynamic because their lives were more adventurous. Not being domesticated themselves, they envisioned God as equally unencumbered by the confinements of settled life. Seen through the window of history, those mighty ancestors traveled like pioneers of the spirit, exciting, romantic, daring, rugged, and heroic. They lived in the age of the giants of religion. When they chose a campsite, they pitched tents for themselves. And they made a tent — or tabernacle — for God's ark in the middle of the encampment. At times, God even "walked" with them when he appeared as a pillar of cloud in the daytime and a pillar of fire at night.

Their descendants in Christ's time hoped to recapture some of that religious dynamism in their eight day festivities of camping out in their leafy tents, singing songs, praising God, eating heartily, telling stories, marching in religious processions, playing games, and catching up on what had happened to their friends and relatives in the past year.

Tabernacles was the most cheerful of all Jewish feasts. Not the most important. That was Passover. Tabernacles was for them what Thanksgiving and the Fourth of July are for Americans, a mixture of patriotism, religion and heartfelt gratitude for the bounty of the earth. This was not a churchy feast, but more of a family festival where faith had a light hearted tone.

Jesus Goes to the Feast (Jn. 7:1-13)

It should be evident to the reader by now that John liked to arrange his gospel narrative about Jesus around the religious feasts of the Jewish calendar. Passover. Jewish Pentecost. Tabernacles. These feasts dealt directly with God's action in history. John's gospel did no less, for he clearly showed how Jesus, the Word become flesh was reshaping history. And what better place was there to underscore this truth than at a liturgical festival?

One vivid connection between Jesus and Tabernacles was the tents. Thousands of people pitched their branch tents in the available spaces in Jerusalem (sometimes on rooftops) and outside its walls. Remarkably, the Word of God had come to earth and "pitched his tent among us." With a heady mix of nostalgia and history, blurred by distance and romanticized by memory, the celebrants encountered in Jesus a new and unexpected realization of the ancient event of tenting in the wilderness. God the Father had walked with their ancestors. God the Son walked with them now, not as a mysterious cloud and fire, but as a visible person and friend. Love had found a way to be present to them in a manner totally unforeseen.

On the eve of the feast, Jesus and his disciples were doing mission work in Galilee. Jesus had stayed away from Judea because the religious leaders had obtained warrants for his arrest and made no secret of their plans to have him killed. They wanted to be rid of this troublesome preacher and wonder worker. The disciples did not realize the seriousness of the situation. Even if popular support for Jesus had waned in Galilee after the Bread of Life discourse, there was still a feeling that Jesus enjoyed considerable acceptance in the mountain villages and the fishing towns along the lakeshore.

Lulled by the pleasant Galilean mission, they did not quite comprehend the depth of hostility Jesus had caused among the powers that be in the south, the bureaucratic center of their religion. Authorities never like having situations and people they cannot control. This is how Jesus seemed to them. His ministry not only disturbed their standard approach to religion, but also was fraught with political dangers. He might upset the uneasy compromises they made with the Roman rulers. A threat to the social and religious order of things must be removed, violently if necessary.

The disciples wanted to be in Jerusalem for all the excitement and enjoyment of Tabernacles. They knew Jesus was reluctant to go. They tried to persuade him by arguing that he needed to let the broader world see how powerful his message was and how wondrous were his works. Jesus knew they still did not grasp the essence of his mission. "His brothers did not believe in him" (verse 5).

He resorted to plain and unsentimental language to instruct them. They did not appreciate the hatred he was attracting from the power of evil in the world. They did not yet experience such hostility because they had not begun to confront the evil that must be identified and fought against. He told them they simply had not yet realized the issue at hand, the conquest of evil and the hatred for those who would battle against it.

Jesus encouraged them to go and enjoy themselves at the feast. His "hour" had not yet come. The real "hour" would be the passion. Here Jesus seems to refer more to the opportunity for effective mission, because in fact he did leave for the feast soon after his disciples had departed. Jesus arrived at Tabernacles in the middle of the festivities when the receptivity to faith in his message would be greater. He was not worried about his safety. He was more concerned about the spiritual health of his beloved people and wanted to open them as much as he could to receiving his offer of salvation.

Send the Temple Police to Arrest Jesus (Jn. 7:14-36)

Jesus arrived in a Jerusalem that was enjoying itself to the full. Tabernacles was at midpoint. The cumulative celebrating had generated a genial atmosphere in which the sacred and the secular purposes had blended to cause a widespread companionable spirit. Jesus proceeded to give some widely admired Scripture lessons. Trained rabbis were astonished that he could be so good at it, considering he had not taken any formal studies in the Bible. Such training consisted in becoming a student of a recognized rabbi, where one studied the opinions of famous rabbis of the past about the texts of Scripture. "How does he know Scripture without having studied?" (verse 15).

The easy mood of the moment made Christ's reply more persuasive. He told them he was trained by a very well known teacher — his heavenly Father. He had attended the best and most prestigious of all rabbinical schools, the classroom of God. Jesus explained that the effectiveness of his Scripture teaching proceeded from a life of obedience to his Father's will and the intention of seeking only God's glory, not one's own. This comment about glory is "presence talk." To seek God's glory is not to conduct religious and musical fireworks to tickle a divine ego. Rather it means to open a window and let God's loving presence be felt.

Thus mastery of Scripture is more than studying texts and famous opinions about them. That is indeed important. But without a life of obedience to God's will and a commitment to unfold his glory presence to the world, the core meaning of Scripture will never be really known. In the last analysis, Bible study is an act of faith.

Suddenly, Jesus broke the pleasant spell of Tabernacles and the mild jousting between himself and his questioners. It was as though a threatening cloud had darkened those sunny moments. Jesus took the initiative and swept away pretenses. "Why are you trying to kill me?" (verse 19). He questioned those religious bureaucrats about their lethal conspiracy. At another level he was putting the Prince of Darkness on notice. It was evil itself which was out to destroy him, for "The Prince" knew that Jesus was determined to remove evil's control over the human heart, not just in these religious leaders but in every person who was subject to evil and sin.

Jesus had shattered the "feel good" mood of Tabernacles. Unaware of the reality of evil's intent against Christ and not informed about the plots of the religious leaders, the people roared out that Jesus was crazy. Who would want to kill him? Their outcry came as much from being irritated at Jesus for raining on their parade as from a genuine disbelief that anyone would even dream of killing him.

Jesus then spoke of the murderous reaction to his healing on the sabbath, something most pilgrims would have known little about.

The discussion turned to the subject of Christ's origins. People were aware that Jesus was being called the messiah by some. They said he could not be the messiah because they knew he came from Nazareth. Such a statement was based on the theory of the "hidden messiah," which claimed that no one could know the origin or birthplace of the messiah. He would appear "out of the blue." That is why some thought Elijah would come again to identify the messiah and anoint him. Another instance of the hidden messiah theory occurred at Caesarea Philippi, where Peter had confessed that Jesus was the messiah. Jesus praised Peter for discovering what had been "hidden" from the eyes of all.

Jesus told them they may know his earthly birthplace, but they did not know about his heavenly origin. They were missing the truth about him both as messiah (Their hidden messiah theory stopped that) and as Son of God.

Aware of his double claim to messiahship and divinity, the religious leaders sent temple police to arrest him. This is the first of two arrest scenes in the gospels, the other being at Gethsemane. In both cases the officers had no ability to touch him until he gave permission — which happened when his "hour" came. The attempts on his life led him to think about his death and his return to his Father after the resurrection.

Wave the Myrtle Branches and Lemons (Jn. 7:37-52)

Practically speaking, the most important aspect of Tabernacles was rain. Ardent prayers for rain were chanted. If rain fell during the feast, it was considered a good omen predicting that more rain will come, much needed for the fertile crops of the following year.

Every morning during the feast a rain procession was held. The pilgrims marched to the spring of Gihon at the foot of temple Mount. This spring supplied the water for the pool of Siloam, a kind of ancient reservoir. The priest filled a golden bowl with water and the people sang, "With joy you will draw water at the fountain of salvation" (Is. 12:3). The people returned to the temple, marching through the Water Gate.

The pilgrims carried myrtle and willow branches tied with palm in their right hands. These symbolized their tents. They carried lemons in their left hands, symbolizing the harvest. Gathered around the altar of holocausts in front of the temple building, they sang various psalms, waved the branches and lemons and swayed to the rhythms of the music. The priest ascended the steps to the altar and poured out the water onto the altar. The gesture imitated the falling of rain, "reminding" God to send real rain.

Amid the drama and color of this rain parade, the music, the gleaming gold of the water bowl, the lemons and myrtle branches — perhaps even an actual autumnal rainfall — Jesus stood up and said, "Let anyone who thirsts, come to me and drink. Whoever believes in me, as Scripture says: 'Rivers of living water will flow from within him' " (Jn. 7:37-8).

The people had prayed for water. Jesus proclaimed their prayers had been answered. He was the real response to their hopes. Tabernacles always meant more than rain. It also contained within itself the hope for a messiah. Zechariah had predicted that living waters would flow from Jerusalem. Jesus announced the living waters were now here. Ezekiel had seen a vision in which a river flowed from a rock underneath the temple. Jesus told his listeners that he was the temple. A river of living water will flow from him. Moses had struck a rock in the desert and water flowed from it. On Calvary a soldier lanced the side of Jesus and water flowed from it.

What is this water? It is both the saving water of baptism and the image of the Spirit whom Jesus would send. There was a long and honored tradition in Scripture which connected water images with the pouring out of the Spirit. Ezekiel linked the sprinkling of water to the outpouring of divine spirit. Jesus had spoken of creating a new person out of water and the Spirit. This is sacramental talk. Earthly water. Divine Spirit. Creation and Creator joined together for a saving purpose.

In this passage we have a third example from John's gospel in which a material element is given strong prominence. At Cana Jesus produced gallons of wine. On a Galilean mountain, Jesus created barrels of bread. At Tabernacles Jesus performed no water miracle, but drew a powerful Gospel message from a rain ceremony where water was on everyone's mind. Bread and Wine would have sacramental significance in the Eucharist. The Water acquired sacramental meaning in baptism.

Admittedly, water imagery is prominent in the Baptist's preaching about baptism and in Christ's dialogue with Nicodemus about spiritual transformation. It is true that water was a central image in the conversion of the Samaritan Woman at Jacob's Well, and it was the backdrop of the healing of the man at the pool of Bethesda. But it is only at Tabernacles that water's vivid imagery and symbolism obtains the fullest force.

One may argue that it was the artistry of John's sure pen that created an incremental portrait of the imagery of water at the service of Christ's preaching and saving ministry. The gradual buildup from the Baptist to Nicodemus to the Samaritan Woman to the Pool of Bethesda to Tabernacles is like the swell of a symphony surging to an emotional climax amid myrtle branches and lemons and music and a golden bowl — and yes, water. And above all, there is Jesus from whom will flow water and the Spirit to wash us joyously in love forever.

Reflection

1. What kind of harvest customs and festivals do we have in our culture?
2. What ancient rituals do I know of which were used to make rain happen? And to find underground water?
3. Why did Judaism and Christianity link cultural harvest customs with religious ceremonies?
4. In what way have I experienced "evil" — not just evil people?
5. Why were Christ's disciples so slow to realize the mortal danger facing Jesus in Jerusalem?
6. What was the theory of the "hidden messiah" and how does it show up in this chapter?
7. Describe the Tabernacles' "Water Procession" and the various symbolism involved.
8. How has John woven the water theme from the Baptist to Tabernacles?
9. In what sense do I experience Jesus as the source of living water for me?
10. When I am filled with Christs' "living water" what responsibilities do I acquire?

Prayer

Jesus, source of the living water of the Holy Spirit, you have "pitched your tent/tabernacle" among us. You bless us with life and love. In a special way, I want to recover my baptismal call and mission, to grow in love, to share my faith, to be a fountain of compassion for others. Through my faith intimacy with you, Jesus, I shall be able to do so.

8   A Compassionate Pillar of Fire

Jesus Saves an Adulteress (Jn. 8:1-11)

More will be heard from Christ's experience at Tabernacles, but only after the story of his merciful treatment of the woman taken in adultery.

Prodded by the religious leaders, a self-righteous mob brought a woman "caught in the act of adultery" to Jesus. They asked him to render a judgement about her.

It was a trap. If he recommended stoning, he officially broke Roman law which reserved to itself the right of capital punishment. He would also lose his reputation as a friend of sinners and a teacher of compassion.

If he rejected stoning, he would break Mosaic law which called for capital punishment of an adulteress.

Jesus responded to their attitudes about the woman, not to their conspiracy to entrap him. His reaction was a two-step procedure.

First by silence. Jesus bent down and started tracing on the ground with his finger. Christian imagination has long speculated about that body talk. Did he write out the sins of her accusers? Was he just doodling? Or was he simply letting silence take its toll? This latter position seems the best interpretation. Jesus used the power of silence to let everyone feel the contrast of their noise, so full of self-righteousness, so keyed up for a potential kill, so committed to the pleasure of discrediting him.

Jesus used the therapy of silence to initiate a reflective mood. He did not respond defensively, accusing them of being unfair to him. He did not scorn them as hypocrites. He did not use a brilliant debater's point to get them off his back. He introduced silence. Their heavy and obscene breathing sounded awkward. His technique was like the sound of one hand clapping. He gave them no hand to clap against.

Only when the dust was literally settled and that little army of moralistic combatants found no way to start a war did Jesus speak to their moral attitudes. Jesus said nothing about the woman's adultery. Still bent down, not looking into their faces, he said words that let them judge themselves. "Let the one among you who is without sin be the first to throw a stone at her" (verse 7). The Greek word *anamartetos* "without sin" can also mean "without a sinful attitude."

What attitudes was he talking about?

(a). Their attitude of using authority only to punish and condemn. Authority should primarily be a positive and creative attitude. Those who possess it should be about the business of "authoring" life and love and justice, to heal and rehabilitate.

(b). Their impersonal attitude toward people. They saw her as a category, not a person. An adulteress, not a human being. She is simply a nameless woman guilty of a moral and civil crime. How different God is. "I have called you by name. . . . Because you are precious in my eyes and glorious, and because I love you" (Is. 43:1,4). God is fond of names because God is fond of people. God will not treat a human being as a category. Neither will Jesus.

(c). Their possible lustful attitude. He did not accuse them of this, but asked them to check their hearts. How pure were they? Had they transcended lust and arrived at a life of chaste love? Why were they exerting so much moral passion about the sexual sin of this woman? Did they have something to hide?

The beauty of this whole scene was that Jesus did not engage those "little murderers" on their own terms, but on his. He deftly changed the focus from the woman to themselves. Who were they? What kind of moral attitudes did they espouse?

One by one they dropped their stones and crept silently away. He was left alone with the woman. St. Augustine visualized the scene with these words, "There remained a great Miseria (misery) and a great Misericordia (mercy)." A miserable woman. A merciful savior. Jesus stood up and looked around. Possibly with a smile he could have said, "Oh! Where did they all disappear to? Look at the rocks. Didn't anyone condemn you?" "No one, sir." "Nor do I condemn you. You may go now. But from now on, avoid this sin" (see verses 10-11).

The duty of a doctor is sometimes to heal, often to give relief and always to console. Jesus treated her with compassion. The duty of an honest person is to tell the truth with love. Jesus told her he knew she had sinned. She realized he had released her from her present problem and its consequences. He had given her a second chance. Jesus challenged her not to sin again. He did not give her easy forgiveness. No cheap grace. He appealed to her capacity for conversion and moral change. He made her feel it was possible. Yes, a sinner can become a saint. It cannot be proved from Scripture, but popular tradition says that the woman was Mary Magdalene. Scripture says she was one of the four friends of Jesus who were brave enough to stand at the foot of the cross.

Maybe it was this same woman.

Jesus, the New Pillar of Fire (Jn. 8:12-20)

In a world without electricity, most people went to bed at sundown. Most people could not afford the oil or wax to keep candles and torches going at night. But at the feast of Tabernacles the night sky was ablaze with festal torches in the Court of the Women on Temple Mount. Four golden candlesticks, each tall enough that ladders were used to reach the tops, were capped with golden bowls of oil, with lighted wicks floating in them.

This extravagance of night fire on the eight evenings of Tabernacles was one of the mystic delights of the feast. It probably had the same effect on those people that fireworks have for moderns, despite the less dramatic form of torchlight. Appointed men danced before the Lord while choirs sang psalms of praise to God, the pillar of fire who had walked with their ancestors in the desert.

Onto this splendid stage walked Jesus. In a pause between the singing and the dancing, Jesus said, "I AM the light of the world. Whoever follows me will not walk in darkness, but will have the light of life" (verse 12). Another "I AM" statement so typical in John's gospel. Jesus told them that the old pillar of fire has become a person living among them. Using the powerful visual aid of the ceremony of fire at Tabernacles, Jesus gave it the meaning it was destined to have.

The early Christians often called baptism the "Illumination." They would naturally have connected this Tabernacles' scene and Christ's self identification as light with baptism. In Chapter 9 of John, the story of the cure of the man born blind will be a natural extension of this scene. Jesus is light. Just as light opposes the darkness of the night, so the light of Jesus dispels the darkness of sin. All religious literature links evil deeds with darkness and graced behavior with light. Christ's guiding light is not simply a candle to find one's way home at night. It is a light that banishes evil from the heart so one can find one's way home to God.

The Pharisees told Jesus that his self-equation with light could not be accepted because there were no witnesses to back him. They could not agree with him on his word alone. Jesus replied that he could very well witness on his own behalf. He knew himself and who he was and where he came from.

At the same time he pointed out that he did indeed have a witness, his heavenly Father. A divine presence and glory permeated his teachings, deeds and impact upon others. The wisdom with which he spoke reflected the presence of God. His acts were windows through which could be seen the divine power. His tremendous ability to change people's lives, especially hardened sinners, was vivid evidence of God's witness to him. His capacity to touch hearts as no other person was a dramatic instance of the Father's loving witness to his Son.

The World (Jn. 8:21-30)

Jesus told his opponents, "You belong to this world, but I do not belong to this world. . . . If you do not believe that I AM, you will die in your sins" (verses 23-4).

The expression "world" often appears in John's gospel. In his usage, the term has a complex meaning.

• This world is not heaven. The world is a passing and transient place. Heaven is a permanent reality. The world symbolizes what is opposed to God.

• But God loves this world. Genesis describes how much love God put into creating it. God loves the world so much that he sent his Son here to save it from evil and sin. Heaven and the world may be different, yet there is a magnificent link between them because of God's affection for people.

• Still, something has gone wrong with the world. It does not recognize Jesus; indeed, it engages in open hostility to him. The world is not what it was meant to be in the original design for creation. The world represents sin, evil and all that breaks people away from a relationship with God.

Jesus has come to solve this impasse. Jesus brought love and forgiveness and reconciliation. God is in Christ reconciling the world to himself.

In recent times there has been an unfounded optimism about the world. And this despite the horrors of Hiroshima, the holocaust, the worst wars in history, widespread poverty, hunger, and injustice. Political systems arose that enslaved half the earth's population, systems that believed a paradise can be created on earth, governments that taught people had no need of God. Jesus would say to this "world" that without God there is no hope of happiness, peace, justice, harmony, a decent way of life, and an environment that supports human dignity.

The only solution to the world as representing evil is the passion and resurrection of Jesus. "When you lift up the Son of Man, then you will realize that I AM" (verse 28). The expression "lift up" refers both to the lifting up of Jesus on the cross and his lifting up to glory in his resurrection from the dead. The only way to regenerate the notion and reality of the "world" is to believe in a supernatural solution. All human effort without God will fail. That was the lesson of the story of the Tower of Babel. It is the lesson Jesus persistently teaches. Divine redemption is the answer for an evil world.

Cry Freedom! Jesus Presents the Real Abraham (Jn. 8:30-59)

Christ's discussion with his opponents moved to the subject of freedom. He told them that he spoke the truth, and this truth would make them free. They replied that they had never been enslaved, so why would he even raise the subject of slavery? There are three kinds of freedom: political, psychological, spiritual. They were thinking only of political and psychological freedom. Even when they were slaves in Babylon, they felt interior freedom. Their present bondage to Rome did not crush their proud inner freedom. Political oppression had never suppressed their sense of psychological freedom.

But Jesus was referring to spiritual freedom. Anyone who committed a sin was a slave to evil, not spiritually and morally free. Only the moral person is really free. The sinner claims to be free because he does what he likes with his life. That is an illusion. The sinner does what sin wants him to do. Pride, lust, envy, anger, gluttony, and avarice are tough slave masters. They are the worst tyrants a soul will ever encounter. Those evil slave drivers cause a human being to self destruct.

A political monster dominates the body and environment of people and causes unspeakable suffering. An interior moral monster does worse. The only one who can conduct an uprising against such a devil is Jesus, the real liberator of the human person. Christ's truth is the best medicine for a sick soul. His truth causes inner freedom from the moral slavery to sin. Jesus reminded them that their intention to murder him was a sign of their spiritual bankruptcy, their enslavement to evil. Cry Freedom! Cry for spiritual freedom!

Because of their slavery to sin, they are not real children of Abraham. They argued that biological descent from Abraham was the source of their national pride, their religious dignity, their very identity as persons. Jesus rejected their claim. The only way to really be a child of Abraham was to act like the great patriarch. Pointing to the rocks, Jesus told them that God could raise descendants of Abraham up from these very stones (see Mt. 3:9)! Abraham had welcomed messengers from God. Jesus was the greatest messenger God ever sent to his people. They wanted to kill him. Is that how a descendant of Abraham acts? Abraham listened with an open heart to the truth from God. They refused to listen to God's messenger, Jesus.

Fighting back, they loudly proclaimed that God was their Father. Jesus replied that if they really meant that, they would accept him. "If God were your Father, you would love me, for I came from God and am here" (verse 42). They would listen to his Gospel if they really believed in God as their Father. Repeatedly, Jesus made it clear that how one reacted to him was the real test of a person's faith. Jesus is central to the world's history and to the life story of every woman and man. People have found all kinds of methods to eliminate Jesus from his key role. They have used murder, rational arguments, ridicule, cynical indifference, financial oppression and other means. But Jesus cannot be ignored. He is the Tremendous Lover who confronts each person with his offer of salvation.

Jesus charged his opponents with being children of the devil. The devil is the author of death and killing. They wanted to kill him. The devil is the father of lies. They cannot accept the truth. They lived by lies. Dramatically he challenged them to find any sin in him. "Can any of you charge me with sin?" (verse 46). They were reduced to frustrated silence. If they can find no evil in him, why were they unable to hear the truth he spoke? Because they were in bondage to the father of lies.

Jesus went on to say that Abraham rejoiced to see his day. There was a tradition that Abraham had received a vision of the whole history of Israel and the coming of the messiah. Jesus claimed that he was the messiah and that Abraham had seen him coming. That was why he rejoiced to see his day. His adversaries argued that Jesus was not yet fifty. How could he have seen Abraham? Fifty years was the retirement age for Levites.

Jesus replied, "Before Abraham came to be, I AM" (verse 58). He did not say, "Before Abraham was, I was." No, "I AM." At this confession of his divinity he departed from the temple area just as the Jews picked up stones to throw at him. The process that would lead to his passion was now in full flood.

Reflection

1. In the story of the woman taken in adultery, what was the trap Christ's adversaries laid for him?
2. Why was Christ's silence, while he doodled in the sand, so effective?
3. How does silent reflection help me to evaluate my moral attitudes?
4. What was the ceremony of light like at Tabernacles?
5. How is Jesus the light of my life?
6. Why is it true to say that the test of my religious faith is my reaction to and relation with Jesus?
7. How is the word "world" used in John's gospel?
8. Why is Christ's passion and resurrection (His being "lifted up") the only real solution to the problem of evil in the world?
9. Today everyone talks about freedom. What kind of freedom are they talking about? Political, psychological or spiritual? How is a sinner a slave to sin?
10. How does Jesus liberate me from the slavery to sin?

Prayer

Jesus, your compassion for the woman taken in adultery is a tremendous story of courage and compassion. Your arguments with your lethal opponents at Tabernacles remind me of how forthright I must be in standing up for my faith. Be my light, dear Lord. Put its fire of spiritual bravery in my heart. Place its clarity of truth in my mind. Carry me with your love that I may be a source of hope to everyone I meet.

9 The Blind Man Sees — Seeing Ones Are Blind

Jesus Heals the Man Born Blind (Jn. 9:1-41)

Everyone has compassion for a physically blind person and admiration for the courage and resourcefulness a blind one shows in taking hold of life. Other types of blindness will cause a negative reaction in us. Moral and spiritual blindness will prevent religious conversion and faith growth and often cause harm to others. Both kinds of blindness appear in John's ninth chapter.

This story as narrated by John lends itself to a dramatic presentation, which we will use to begin this chapter. The reflection will follow this imaginative reconstruction of the sequence of events.

The Miracle

John: See that blind beggar. I hear he has been on this corner for years.

Philip: I spent some time with him yesterday. He's a crusty character. He pushed his way to this spot where he could be near the most pilgrims to the temple. Told me that he has been blind from birth.

John: A pity. I wonder what sin caused his problem.

Philip: Jesus, do you think this man's blindness was due to his own sin?

Jesus: If that were so, Philip, he would have to have sinned when he was in his mother's womb. Can you believe that?

Philip: I suppose not. Well then, was it his parents' sin?

Jesus: I'm not sure we want to stand here and discuss the mystery of evil and its effects while this poor man suffers. Through him God's glory-presence will be experienced.

(Jesus bends down and begins to mix his saliva with the clay.)

John: Master, what are you doing?

Jesus: Watch. . . . Sir, let me put this paste on your eyes. I want to heal you.

Blind Man: All right. Others have tried. But I'm always hopeful.

Jesus: Go to the Pool of Siloam and wash away the mud from your eyes. You will see for the first time in your life. (He went off and washed and came back able to see.)

The Investigations —
Neighbors and Friends Question the Beggar

A Neighbor: Isn't he the one who used to be a beggar?

A Shop Owner: No. Just looks like him, that's all.

Blind Man: I'm the one. I've been healed.

Neighbor: Amazing! How did it happen?

Blind Man: You have heard of Jesus. He upset a lot of people at the Tabernacles festival. Well he made some mud, smeared it on my eyes. Told me to go to Siloam and wash the mud off. At that moment I could see. I could see!

Shop Owner: Where's Jesus now?

Blind Man: I have no idea.

(Pharisees examine him)

Pharisee: How is that you can see?

Blind Man: Jesus put mud on my eyes. I washed them. Now I see.

Pharisee: He did this on the sabbath?

Blind Man: Yes.

Pharisee: He broke the sabbath law on work.

Scribe: Such a man cannot be from God.

Pharisee: Still, how can he be a sinner and yet perform such miracles? He healed you, sir. What do you think of him?

Blind Man: That's easy. He's a Prophet.

The Jews Opposed to Jesus Interrogate the Beggar's Parents

A Jew: Is this your son?

Mother: Yes.

A Jew: Was he born blind?

Father: Yes.

A Jew: We don't believe you. It's impossible that this happened.

Mother: I'm his mother. I should know. It broke my heart.

Father: Look, this is our son. Of course we know he was born blind. We have no idea how he was cured. Ask him. He is old enough to speak for himself. We don't want any trouble about our membership in the synagogue.

Pharisees' Second Interrogation of the Blind Man

Pharisee: Honor God with the truth. Declare that Jesus is a sinner.

Blind Man: How would I know that he is a sinner? Listen carefully to me. I'll say it slow. I was blind. Now I see.

Scribe: How could he have done this? What did he do?

Blind Man: I may have been blind. You seem to be deaf and your condition is getting worse. I already told you how he did it. You don't pay attention.... Wait! I know why you want to hear the story again. You want to be his disciples.

A Jew: Never! You are his disciple. We follow Moses not this charlatan. We know that God spoke to Moses. We have no confidence in this faker.

Blind Man: Jesus is a kind man.

Pharisee: He's a sinner.

Blind Man: You people are crazy. Everyone in the street knows that God does not listen to sinners. God pays attention to good people who obey his will. No one ever heard of someone curing a man *born* blind. I tell each and everyone of you this man is from God. That's why he could cure me.

Scribe: You were born steeped in sin! You have a nerve lecturing us!

Pharisee: Throw him out of here!

Jesus Gives Him Spiritual Sight

Jesus: Did they give you a hard time?

Blind Man: Don't worry. I knew how to handle them. I've been a fighter since I was a child.

Jesus: Do you believe in the Son of Man?

Blind Man: Tell me who he is. I want to believe in him.

Jesus: You are looking at him with your new found sight. I invite you to look with faith.

Blind Man: I do believe, Lord. (And he bowed to worship Jesus.)

The blind beggar of this story comes across as a tough and seasoned man. Blind from birth he has made the best of his life. He is a man of character. His disability has made him street smart. No one is going to push him around, as became evident in his sharp exchange with the Pharisees.

He must have been a well known figure near the temple area, having claimed his begging spot with a combination of aggressiveness and seniority among the local mendicants. The encounter with Jesus and the apostles may have taken place during Tabernacles. At that feast, Jesus had said he was the world's light. In a very complete way he would prove this by healing the total person of the blind man, his physical eyes and the eyes of his soul.

The apostles noted that the man had been blind from birth. Was that due to his own sins or those of his parents? Popular religion of the time held that illness and disease were punishments for sins. If you were born with an affliction, it was assumed that the sins of your parents were responsible. "I, the Lord, your God, am a jealous God, inflicting punishment for their fathers' wickedness on the children of those who hate me"(Ex. 20:5). However, there was an eccentric, minority opinion that even a baby in the womb was capable of sin, in which case the unborn child was the cause of the misfortune. Following this view, the blind man could have sinned prior to birth and so incurred his loss of sight.

Jesus did not try to explain the link between sin and suffering. He said that this man's problem was an occasion for illustrating what God can do. In the synoptic gospels, miracles were signs of God's compassion for human suffering. In John's gospel, they reveal God's glory-presence to human awareness.

These are complementary, not contradictory purposes. One may think of the God of compassion as still very far away from everyday life. John's teaching makes it clear that the divine miracle worker is as near as the warm touch of a healing hand. Miracles in the synoptics looked at the *joyful results in the healed.* Miracles in John observed the *people's joyful experience of the healer.* One looked at the outcome. The other looked at the cause.

Jesus then reminded them of what he had just said at Tabernacles. He was the light of the world. He proceeded to spit on the ground and make some mud from the clay. He smeared the mud paste on the blind man's eyes and told him to go and wash them in the Pool of Siloam. The man did so and received the gift of sight.

Three times in the gospels Jesus used saliva to effect a cure, here in John, again in the case of the deaf stutterer in Mark 7:33, and of another blind man in Mark 8:22-26. Folk medicine of the time believed in the therapeutic value of saliva, especially that of a famous person. Even today if we burn or cut our finger, our first impulse is to lick it or put it in our mouths.

Jesus did not need to use saliva or call for a ritual washing in a pool. Most of the time he healed simply by saying a few words. But he was also conscious of the human need of the person to have confidence in him. If he acted like a doctor at times that was to minister to a psychological need, not because he was compelled to use such methods to heal.

The Pool of Siloam was the result of a remarkable engineering feat of ancient times. In the Kedron Valley outside the city walls there was a spring named Gihon, or the Virgin's Fountain. In the time of the Jewish monarchy, an underground pipe was laid from the spring to a pool inside the city. This secret, concealed water supply would help the inhabitants of the city to withstand a siege. The pool was an open air basin about twenty by thirty feet. It was called Siloam (or sent) because it received the water "sent" to it by the Virgin's Spring. It was at this pool the blind man obtained his sight after he washed the mud from his eyes. Recall also that it was from this pool the priest drew water for the "prayer for rain" procession at Tabernacles.

After the healing there are four episodes in which a questioning or scrutiny takes place. These incidents mark four stages of spiritual growth in the healed man and four steps leading from doubt to militant disbelief on the part of the Jews. When John speaks of "the Jews" he is not talking of all Jews, but of those who were actively antagonistic to Jesus and his followers.

By the time this gospel was written, the sharp break between the Christian and Jewish communities had occurred. The heated disputes between Jesus and the religious leaders and those whom John calls "the Jews" were repeated in the early church as the two faiths parted ways. The passion evident in the gospel confrontations were all too well known in the infant church. These texts about "the Jews" should not be used for anti-semitic purposes. Christians should not be anti-semitic for any reason. The Gospel is meant to foster unity between and among all peoples under God's Fatherhood.

The following chart captures the four stages of faith and disbelief just mentioned. The man in the dark comes gradually to the light both physically and spiritually. And those opposed to Jesus gradually sink into the darkness of disbelief.

The Enlightenment of the Ignorant

Blind Man	His Faith Growth
1. Questioned by neighbors.	It was a MAN called Jesus.
2. Questioned by Pharisees.	Jesus is a PROPHET.
3. Questioned again by Pharisees.	Miracle proves Jesus is FROM GOD.
4. Questioned by Jesus.	Worships Jesus as SON Of MAN.

The Ignorance of the Enlightened

Pharisees/The Jews	Their Disbelief Growth
1. First Questioning	They accept the healing. Some willing to be convinced.
2. Second Questioning	Now hostile to Jesus. Doubt a miracle happened.
3. Questioning His Parents.	Assert he was never even blind.
4. Last Interrogation of Man.	No interest in truth. They try to convict the witness of lying.

The cured man displayed increasing insight. First, he viewed Jesus as just a man. Second, he perceived him as a prophet like the miracle workers of ancient times. Third, as one from God, for who else would be behind so wonderful a deed? Lastly, he revered Jesus as Son of Man.

The Jews opposed to Jesus demonstrated a descent into cynical disbelief. They began by accepting the miracle, then doubting it, next even doubting the man was ever blind. Lastly, they discredited the testimony of the man and basically expressed their refusal to believe Jesus.

This was a contest between humility and pride, between insight and closed minds, between light and darkness. It was like the difference between people who know they do not know everything and those who think they know it all. Wisdom is the reward for the humble. Empty ignorance is the outcome for the proud. The blind man confessed his ignorance three times. Yet he was growing in knowledge of Jesus. He started in darkness and arrived at the light. The Pharisees three times boast they know all about Jesus, but progressively lapse into ignorance about him. They began in the light and ended up in darkness.

The Baptismal Character of the Story

We have already noted that early Christians called baptism the Illumination or Enlightenment. Catacomb art used this story seven times, most often as a picture of Christian baptism. Early Christian catechists employed this story as a reading to prepare converts for baptism. In a further historical development the reading was incorporated in the "great scrutiny" — a final exam for baptism. When the candidates had been finally judged ready for baptism, Old Testament readings about cleansing waters were read to them.

Next occurred the formal opening of the gospel book. John, chapter 9 was read, ending with the healed blind man's confession of faith, "I do believe, Lord" (verse 38). Echoing his faith, the candidates recited the Creed. The use of saliva to anoint the eyes eventually became part of the baptismal ritual, reflecting yet another influence of the story on the sacramental ceremony.

A baptismal theme is found within the story itself. Jesus told the man to wash in the Pool of Siloam, which means "sent," reminding the reader that Jesus so often spoke of being sent to us by the Father. The water will have healing power, just as baptismal water does by the power of the Spirit. The water from that pool was used at Tabernacles as a symbol to ask God for the creative rains that would cause new growth in the future. Jesus had stood front and center for that ceremony and identified himself as the real life giving water, a water that in sacramental terms would be baptism.

This fine, well crafted story is clearly filled with wise

observations about spiritual growth based on openness to Jesus and spiritual decline founded on having a closed mind toward Jesus. It demonstrates that faith in Jesus will result in commitment to him, one that will culminate in the reception of baptism.

Only a Jesus centered faith that leads to baptism in a church community assures the kind of Christian spiritual growth envisioned by the Gospel. Some people want a Christianity without Christ, which results in a religion with no faith requirement and no moral demands. Jesus is offstage longer here than in any gospel text. Those who wish to keep him off fall into radical disbelief. The same thing happens today even within religion. People try to distract others from thinking of Jesus, praying to him, believing in him, being near him in the sacraments, especially Eucharist. The result will be a loss of faith.

The scrappy, street smart blind man of this story is the perfect antidote to any effort to blindside the faithful from contact with Jesus. This nameless man is the patron saint of Christian realists. His stubborn loyalty to Jesus opened him to strong faith. We have much to learn from him for our own faith journey.

Reflection

1. This story shows that the people connected sin with illness. What were times in my life when I believed my sinful behavior caused me physical illness or emotional depression?
2. What did Jesus mean when he said the blind man was an occasion for experiencing the glory-presence of God?
3. What is the difference in purposes for the miracles in the synoptic gospels and those in John?
4. How can I see the evolution of faith in the blind man? What did he do to prove it?
5. How can I show the decline of faith in the Jews opposed to Jesus from this story?
6. What details from the story show a connection with Tabernacles?
7. Why did Jesus use the mud paste to cure the man? What was the baptismal significance of washing in the Pool of Siloam?
8. What other connections with baptism do I see in this story?
9. What do I learn from the story to strengthen my personal commitment to Jesus?

10. How does the story help me with my baptismal faith?

Prayer

Jesus, light of the world and living water, you applied your public witness at Tabernacles in your ministry to the man born blind. You became his light and the living water of salvation for him. You are the same for me, enlightening my mind and washing my heart clean from evil. Like the blind man, I confess my faith in you, adore you for your love and pledge to live out the implications of my baptism. Stay with me on my faith journey and help me to be a light to others.

10   Good Shepherd, Home Again You Brought Me

The Shepherd Psalm 23 is the most beloved of all the psalms. It must have been a favorite of Jesus as well, for he loved to use the image of the shepherd. Jesus was a master of Scripture. He did more than pray this psalm. He embodied its vision and lived out its dream. Before reflecting on this Good Shepherd chapter, we will review the beautiful words of Psalm 23 and then see how it was used by Jesus. The shepherds of Spain have handed down a traditional interpretation of this psalm based on their own experience with their flocks. Their touching words will guide us here.

The opening verse, "The Lord is my shepherd, I shall not want," speaks about the trusting attitude of the sheep. Instinctively, they know the shepherd will care for them. Christ is our shepherd who loves us. Our response to him should be one of trust based on the conviction Jesus will always care for us.

The psalm continues, "He makes me lie down in green pastures." The grazing habits of sheep are strictly structured. At 3:30 in the morning they begin eating and continue until 10:00 a.m. when they rest. The shepherd directs them first to the rough herbage, then to the smoother grass, and finally to the rich, fine, sweet grass of the green pasture. Then he "makes them lie down" contentedly in the verdant pasture.

Jesus feeds us first with the rough herbage of challenging Christian ideals. He does not give us a soft religion, but one that opens us to the difficulties of loving others, serving their needs, struggling for justice, alleviating the needs of the poor, feeding the hungry, visiting the sick, consoling the hurting people, and conquering evil. But he knows we also need the smoother grass of affirmation. He touches our hearts with his affection, assuring us that he loves us and expressing his delight with our moral commitments. Lastly, he makes us lie down in green pastures, knowing that we need the quiet of prayer and the rest of contemplation where our souls are renewed by the stream of power from his divine energy.

Sheep will not drink from running streams. Hence the verse, "Beside restful waters he leads me." The shepherd must often construct little pools of still water so the sheep may drink. Jesus knows we will not find refreshing water on the fast track of modern life. Our fast pace will never satisfy the deeper thirst of our spirits. Call it the parched throat of the soul or psychological burn-out, the result is the same. Jesus brings us to stillness which permits us to drink from the renewing inner fountains of grace. He announced that gift at Tabernacles and delivers on his promise by being himself the source of that restful water.

Everyone knows the next verse, so familiar, so consoling. "Even though I walk through the valley of the shadow of death, I fear no evil, for you are with me." There is a valley of the shadow of death in Palestine. It is a narrow pass, four miles long, stretching from Jerusalem to the Dead Sea. The walls of the valley are 1,500 feet high. The width seldom exceeds fifteen feet.

Only one path cuts through it, barely a foot wide. Twice a year the shepherd takes his flocks through it because of a change in climate. The sheep encounter three dangers. First, a small ravine breaks the path midway through the valley. The sheep must be coaxed to leap over it. Sometimes the shepherd carries the mother sheep across it so the lambs will be encouraged to jump it to be with her. If they fall, the shepherd uses the curved end of his staff to pull them out.

The second danger is the pointed rocks which menace the sheep on all sides. The last problem is the wild dogs and wolves who prowl the valley. The lead sheep gives a signal should they appear. The shepherd rushes forward, using the pointed end of his staff to drive away or kill the enemy. If sheep could speak in this situation, they might say: "Your rod and your staff. They comfort me."

We always walk in the shadow of death no matter our age. Babies die of crib death. Drunken drivers kill children. Teenagers commit suicide. Joggers are killed in dark parks. Vacationers and business travelers die in plane crashes. Young men die in wars and young women die of drugs. Cancer, heart trouble and old age beckon death.

Jesus knows the shadow of death lies over the whole human race. He accepted his own death as the price of being human. He endured a violent death to save us from sin and to conquer death itself. Like the shepherd in the psalm he saves us from life's major dangers. We all come to ravines across which we must jump. He is with us to give us the courage. Should we fall, he uses the curved end of his staff — the Sacrament of Reconciliation — to pull us up so we can start again.

For each of us life is full of pointed rocks, whose sharp edges rough us up, annoy us, wear us down. Jesus stays with us urging us forward despite the wearing nuisances of living. Lastly, the wild dogs and wolves of evil and sin want to eat us, consume our spiritual strength, and enslave us to self destructive behavior. We cannot hope to fight off the forces of evil alone. We just do not have sufficient spiritual resources because we are fundamentally weakened by original sin. Jesus came precisely to be the "extra added ingredient," the spiritual power that makes it possible for us to overcome sin and evil. The iron-hard end of his staff will drive away the forces of evil and deliver us. Why else do we pray, "Deliver us from evil." What other words could console us more effectively?

"Jesus, your rod and your staff. They comfort me."

At night, the sheep enter, one by one, into the sheepfold. There is only one opening. The walls of the enclosure are made of rocks piled on one another and topped with thorn bushes to keep out predatory animals. The shepherd inspects each one for cuts and fever. Any sheep wounded that day by rocks or thorns is anointed with oil. Then, to cool the fever of any animal, the shepherd plunges the head of the sheep into a basin of cool water to lower the temperature. Thus the meaning of the next verse .

"You anoint my head with oil. My cup overflows."

Jesus will say that he is the gate of the sheepfold. There is no door for the enclosure. The shepherd lies down at the one opening, becomes the living door to the fold. He guards them with his body. To enter the community of Christ the beloved, we must go through him whose body serves as the gate to happiness. He inspects each one of us for the cuts of sin and a fever of passions. He plunges our heads into the cool waters of baptism to allay the fevers of passions that have imprisoned us in sin. He anoints our cuts of sin with the oil of Confirmation that we may have divine courage to withstand all evil. So he makes it possible for goodness and kindness to be our goals all the days of our lives. .

Jesus is the Shepherd of the Shepherd Psalm (Jn. 10:1-18)

As we read the first eighteen verses of the tenth chapter of John we can see how Jesus applied to himself the matchless verses of Psalm 23. As the Word of God he inspired the author of those imperishable words. In his years of growth at Nazareth, tutored by Mary and his "Abba" heavenly Father, he sang those verses and envisioned how they could be lived out here on earth.

He taught that he was the only opening to the community of love, the only door to the Kingdom. His body lay across the opening, just as shepherds would do that night in all the hills of Galilee. A good shepherd knows his sheep by name. He might call one "black ear" or another "brown leg." The sheep know his voice and will not respond to the call of a stranger. H. V. Morton writes that Palestinian shepherds talk to their sheep in a sing-song voice in a language seemingly invented just for this communication. Almost animal like. If the shepherd lets them drift away for a while, he calls them back with a strange laughing noise that has them flocking back to him.

Jesus knows each of us by name, certainly by our baptismal name when we were made his followers. Through prayerful communion with him we begin to "hear" his voice, affectionate, affirming, ready to feed us with the life of the Spirit. This is most evident in the lives of the saints who converse so intimately with Christ, relaxed and at home with him. Just as we need to tune our ears to hear the harmonies and melodies of great symphonies, so we must attune our hearing to the voice of Christ. He does speak. But we must have ears to hear. Jesus repeated, "I am the gate" (verse 7). "Through him we both have access in one Spirit to the Father" (Eph. 2:18). A shepherd gave his sheep the freedom to go in and go out without fear. Jesus does the same. "Whoever enters through me will be saved, and will come in and go out and find pasture" (verse 9). In this age of locked doors, iron bars on windows and security systems, we all know what it means to be afraid. We do not have as much freedom "to go in and go out" as we would like. It is a blessing to have freedom from fear. What we must fear most is becoming a slave of our passions and sinfulness. Jesus assures us that he can deliver us from this worst of human ills. He will give us the freedom to "go in and go out," liberated from sin.

Throughout this passage Jesus frequently referred to "strangers," "hirelings" and "wolves." These are the false shepherds. The strangers will charm us away from our Christian faith. They will promise the goodies of this world in exchange for the graces of Christ. They promise us happiness, but deliver us to despair, like the drug dealers who lurk at the edges of children's playgrounds. Whether it be a killing on the stock market, another extra-marital fling, one more drink for the road, the lottery ticket, the horse that will finally win — the whole thing is a vast illusion from the greatest of all hypnotists, the "stranger," the world that kids us in order to enslave us. Jesus warns us against listening to the voice of the stranger who does not have our own best interests at heart. The second voice comes from the "hireling." This person takes care of the sheep so long as there is not much trouble associated with it. If the wolves come, the hireling will run away and leave the sheep to the mercy of the predators. A real shepherd works for love. The hireling works only for money. Only love has the spirit to protect people. Love is the substance of courage. The shepherds of the church come in many forms: pope, bishops, priests, nuns, parents, teachers. If they are just hirelings, then the church will have sheep without shepherds. The wolves will come and consume them.

The world — in the sense of the unredeemed world — is no friend of Jesus, no friend of Christianity. It is the wolf. When the shepherds of our homes, schools and parishes become merely hirelings, then the wolf has a feast. Real shepherds are brave. They defend their people even at the cost of their lives. Jesus states the principle by which a good shepherd must live. "I will lay down my life for the sheep" (verse 15).

Sometimes the wolf is inside the church, a wolf in sheep's clothing. This is more dangerous because the enemy is less recognizable. Instead of voicing an obvious temptation or roaring a fearful threat, this wolf is like the cunning serpent. Seduction is then the name of the game. Evil is made to seem like goodness. Lies assume the mantle of church teaching. Unwary people buy this food and discover they are poisoned. They become sick before they realize what happened. They are drugged by the pill in the attractive package. Our secularized society can — and sometimes does — infiltrate the pulpits, classrooms, and homes of our parishes and dioceses as the wolf in sheep's clothing. We must be awake and aware of this kind of bad shepherd who can destroy us.

Decide to Love (Jn. 10:17-18)

Why does the Father love Jesus? Because Jesus made his whole life an act of obedience to his Father. He did not do whatever he liked. He did what he should have done. He never separated glory from the cross. "I lay down my life in order to take it up again" (verse 17). He faced death willingly. He absolutely anticipated victory over death. He will take up his life again. He was not being pushed around by determinisms, not in the inner drives of his passions, not the course of history, not the social forces in Galilee and Judea. He acted in magnificent freedom. That is why he was such a terrific shepherd.

And that is what every shepherd in the church is called to be.

Hanukkah — The Festival of Lights (Jn. 10:22-42)

The time was winter.

As evening fell, the cold was relieved by countless pinpoints of light for eight days. Candles and oil lamps glowed from the windows of every home. This was the one time when people indulged in this extravagance. Some families could even afford the *Menorah*, a seven branched candlestick, similar to its giant original version at the temple. In December, the Jews celebrated — as they do today — Hanukkah, the Festival of Lights, also called the Dedication. Once again John situates a teaching of Jesus against the background of a liturgical feast, this time the Dedication.

We can trace its history to the reign of a Syrian King, Antiochus Epiphanes, 175-164 BC. He was overly fond of Greek culture, religion and philosophy and determined that the Jewish people should adopt it. They absolutely refused to accept a new religion and also rejected aspects of Greek culture which they found abhorrent. At first he tried persuasion and then force.

He sent in the troops and started a reign of terror. The death penalty was imposed on anyone who circumcised a child, or had a copy of the Law (first five books of the Bible). Jewish religion was to be exterminated. Rooms at the temple were used for prostitution. A statue of Zeus was installed on the altar of holocausts. The king plundered the gold of the temple and took all the money in the treasury.

The people revolted. In a six year war, Judas Maccabeus and his brother mounted a bloody campaign which they finally won in 164 BC. The temple was cleansed and purified, the altar rebuilt and all that was needed for liturgy restored. The feast of the Dedication recalls this event. It became customary for every family to put a light in the window in memory of this achievement of religious and political freedom.

During this feast, Jesus once again witnessed his message and identity authoritatively in the temple. "The Father and I are one" (verse 30). His unity with the Father was one of perfect love and perfect obedience. His claim aroused murderous feelings in his opponents and they picked up stones to kill him for what they considered to be blasphemy.

Jesus asked them to name the good *works* for which they wanted to stone him. They wanted to kill him for his *words*, his "blasphemous" claim. Jesus granted that they might be blinded by his words, but surely his deeds should give them a different point of view. He healed the sick, fed the hungry, and soothed those who were hurting. Did not such goodness originate from God? Is not loving behavior a window through which shone the divine presence? As he stood that evening by the Menorah, the golden glow of the seven candles bathed him in warmth. But they could not see the Good Shepherd or the Light of the World. They saw only an enemy who must be killed.

Reflection

1. Which verse of the Shepherd Psalm (23) do I like best?
2. In religious terms, when is "my cup overflowing"?
3. What is the "valley of the shadow of death" for me?
4. In my shepherding, how do I know mine, and mine know me?
5. How is Jesus the "gate" of the sheepfold?
6. Why is the hireling not a good shepherd?
7. What exemplifies the ultimate courage of a good shepherd?
8. What is the history behind Hanukkah, the Feast of Dedication?
9. What experiences have I had where people attack me for my words and pay no attention to my good deeds?
10. What happens when homes, schools, parishes and dioceses do not have good shepherds?

Prayer

Jesus, Good Shepherd, I confess that I have strayed often from my loving relationship with you. I have not listened for your voice. Yet you have always called for me. You have pleaded with me to come home. I have resisted your love and followed the charms of hirelings despite the emptiness of their promises and the self destructive dead ends to which they take me. Take me home again. I am ready.

11   Lazarus! Come Out of the Grave!

A death in the family. A death of a friend.

Everyone of us will experience this. Thomas Gray's "Elegy in a Country Churchyard" states that the paths of glory lead but to the grave. Our materialistic culture wants to deny death and hide it from public attention. Yet everyday the newspaper carries an obituary column, stories about murders, fatal accidents, assassinations, suicides, wars, executions, lethal tragedies of all kinds.

Secular philosophers pronounce death absurd, but proceed to draw from death the principle, "Live life to the fullest." Revolutions in medical science have created life support systems that raise new moral and legal debates about the limits of prolonging life. What constitutes "extraordinary means" in this technological age? Death raises financial questions about writing wills, the costs of funerals, cemetery plots, and the advisability of cremation. Death reaches into every aspect of life: religious, moral, financial, legal, philosophical, and social.

It is better to think about death than to deny it. Death should never be an "X-rated topic." One person may look at death and see in it a challenge to make meaning out of life. Another will ponder death and be motivated to expand life's possibilities. Yet again someone will meditate on death and discover deep reserves of hope within the human spirit.

The poet Dylan Thomas looked at death and said that we should not go gentle into that good night. We should "rage, rage against the dying of the light." Those words capture our survival instincts and speak to everyone's profound will to hold onto life. Yet this poet also echoed one of the greatest of biblical teachings:

And death shall have no dominion
Dead men naked, they shall be one
With the man in the wind and the west moon. . .

Though they sink through the sea, they shall rise again.

St. Paul said it of Jesus this way, "Death no longer has power over him" (Rom. 6:9). An even better text is Paul's entire fifteenth chapter of his First Letter to the Corinthians, where he lyrically celebrates the revelation of Christ's resurrection and our own.

Facing the reality of death will be easier when we take seriously its impact on helping us live our lives to the full. Looking death in the face becomes even more valuable when we see it as a door to eternal life, a transition from this form of life to the next. Our funeral liturgy states that life is changed, not taken away. Some of today's self help literature promises happiness through techniques that deter us from looking squarely at pain, tragedy, and death. Instead of going through the sorrow, we are encouraged to run around it. This approach views life as a *headache* quickly cured by an aspirin. But much of life is a *heartache*, not easily remedied by a technique pill.

Death is a teacher whose ultimate lesson is that we cannot run away from problems. Just as we cannot avoid death, neither can we dodge responsibilities and agonies. And when looked at with faith, death also teaches there is another life ahead of us. This is the magnificent lesson of John's account of the resurrection of Lazarus. Christ's stupendous miracle forecasts his permanent resurrection from the dead which he will experience at Easter and make possible for all of us.

Jesus Hears of the Death of Lazarus (Jn. 11:1-16)

When Jesus cured the man born blind, he demonstrated that he was indeed the *Light* of the world.

When he raised Lazarus from the dead he made concrete his claim to be the *Life* of the world.

Three of Jesus' dearest friends were Martha, Mary, and their brother Lazarus from the village of Bethany. This community is just on the other side of the Mount of Olives about two miles from Jerusalem. Bethany means "house of poverty." Lazarus had contracted a serious illness and his sisters sent a message to Jesus about this. Jesus replied that his friend's illness would not end with death. It would become an occasion for the greatest manifestation of the Word's glory-presence, first in the resurrection of Lazarus and above all in the cross.

In John's gospel the supreme revelation of the glory-presence of the Word become flesh takes place at the cross. The lifting up to death, becomes also his lifting up to resurrected life. Sequentially, the death comes first and then the resurrection, but even in the dying and death of Jesus, the Love of God is felt profoundly. From the cross radiated the irresistible glory of God. That is why the suffering and the poor of every age have stood at the cross. They see God already in the crucified. They feel the identity of God with all human tragedy.

John makes it clear that Jesus has a special affection for Martha, Mary, and Lazarus. He loved them. Yet he delayed going to see them for two days. Jesus thereby will dispel all doubt about the death of Lazarus. He will have been buried. Not in a coma. He would have been dead a long enough time so that rabbinic authorities would have said his soul had left his body and decay would definitely have begun. The Lazarus miracle, therefore, will be a sign that Jesus is the source of the life evident in his resurrection.

When Jesus finally announced that they would go to Judea, the apostles objected that it was too dangerous. He had just escaped a stoning threat at the Dedication festival. Why put himself in danger? He replied with a rhetorical question. "Are there not twelve hours in a day?" (verse 9). Yes, there is time each day to accomplish our goals *and* God's will. The flow of time is inexorable. We can waste it. We can use it profitably. By the Incarnation, Jesus accepted the limitations of time, but also filled his allotted time with obedience to his Father's will.

Next came a typical Johannine conversation. Jesus says something that has a double meaning. His listeners misunderstand him. He then clarifies his meaning. He said that Lazarus was asleep. The apostles replied that if he were just resting, there was no reason to be alarmed or to endanger Christ's security. Jesus cleared up their misunderstanding by saying bluntly, "Lazarus has died" (verse 14). John notes that Thomas, who had a second name in Greek — Didymus, meaning twin — touchingly roused the group with his exhortation, "Let us go also and die with him" (verse 16). He was beginning to understand that witnessing to Jesus through personal, courageous behavior was the key to being credible when preaching Christ's message. His heart was in the right place, but like all the apostles, save John, he would falter during the passion and become the most prominent apostolic doubter of the resurrection. Still, by the grace of Jesus, Thomas would be brought to faith and use words often prayed ever since by the devout when adoring Christ in the Blessed Sacrament, "My Lord and my God."

The Mourning Martha Meets Jesus (Jn. 11:17-27)

By the time Jesus arrived at the tomb of Lazarus, his friend had been in the tomb four days. Burial followed death swiftly in that climate. The body was wrapped in a shroud and laid in a niche in a room carved from rock. Sweet spices and oils were applied to the corpse to offset the smell of decay. A round stone was rolled against the door of the grave.

Women led the funeral procession. Usually, some memorial talks were given at the grave. The friends stood in two lines outside the grave as the mourning family members left the tomb and walked between them back to their home. Friends brought prepared foods for a funeral meal after the burial. The official mourning period was seven days. The family stayed at home, receiving a constant stream of visitors and gifts of food. Often Jewish families do the same today, calling this custom "sitting shiva."

Jesus would have come on the scene in the middle of the mourning period. The ever active Martha left the house to meet Jesus, while Mary stayed there. She said to him, "Lord, if you had been here, my brother would not have died. Even now, I know whatever you ask of God, God will give you" (verse 22). There is a tone of reproach in her words. Why did he wait? Why was he so late in coming? At the same time she displayed a remarkable faith in him that he could reverse what had happened.

Once again we have the Johannine conversation. Jesus told her that Lazarus will rise again. Misunderstanding him, she replied that she knew he would rise on the last day. The Pharisees taught this doctrine in opposition to the disbelief of the Sadducees. This teaching about resurrection arose late in Jewish history, around the second century before Christ. It was widely accepted by the common people of Christ's time.

Jesus cleared up what he meant. "I AM the resurrection and the life. Whoever believes in me, even if he die, will live" (verse 25). Martha thought of resurrection as a long postponed event in the misty future of the world's end. She did not realize that the resurrection stood before her. Jesus is not talking about a series of reincarnations into successive life forms, but a unique one-time resurrection from the dead. He will die. So also will Christians and all people. Faith in him will bring a resurrection to eternal life. The intensity of this revelation, so new and so startling, evoked a confession of faith from Martha, one that sounded just like Peter's at Caesarea Philippi. "I have come to believe you are the messiah, the Son of God" (verse 27). The Martha who had been "busy about many things" showed she was truly capable of extraordinary faith.

Mary Meets Jesus — And Then, the Miracle (Jn. 11:28-44)

Mary is brought to see Jesus. She repeats the same words as her sister. Up to this point, the text deals with death in solemn discourse, doctrinal teaching and faith statements. Only when Mary comes and kneels at the feet of Jesus and weeps do we get the feeling we are with a grieving family. Finally Jesus was portrayed as being "perturbed and deeply troubled" (verse 34). When he saw tomb, Jesus responded with grief. "And Jesus wept" (verse 35).

Jesus was able to feel with Martha and Mary the sense of loss they were experiencing. He himself had lost a friend and openly showed his sorrow. As he looked at the grave "an involuntary groan burst from him and he trembled with deep emotion."[*] Jesus was capable of the deepest feelings and unashamed to make them known. He knew how to mourn and to console those who needed his presence and personal strength.

In his *Confessions*, St. Augustine wrote of his difficulty in expressing grief at the death of his mother Monica. "Sorrow flowed into my heart and would have overflowed into tears. But my eyes, under my mind's strong constraint, held back their flow. I stood dry eyed."

He went on to say that his friends stayed with him, but wondered if he lacked all human feeling. "I was ashamed that these human emotions should have power over me." It took him several days

---

[*]Barclay, William, *The Gospel of John*, Vol. 2 (Philadelphia: Westminster Press, 1975), p. 96.

before he was able to permit himself to show sorrow. When he did, he said, "I found consolation in weeping."

Jesus wept for his dear friend Lazarus and out of compassion for Martha and Mary. He also "shuddered, moved with the deepest emotion."[*] at the very fact of death and the reality of sin that brought death into the world. In coming to terms with death and his own reaction to it at the grave of Lazarus, Jesus was even more determined to rid the world of sin and its consequences.

His solution was a love that would conquer death. As he stood at the door of Lazarus' tomb, weeping, the onlookers said, "See how he loved him" (verse 36). How right they were. Jesus' love surged within him and outward to the grave. Love rose from his heart like the waves from the sea. That love assumed resurrection power and informed his voice as he roared at death, "Lazarus, come forth!" And Lazarus emerged from the grave.

Jesus performed a miracle that foreshadowed his own resurrection as well as ours. All such resurrections can only come after going through the experience of death. Jesus would have his own Good Friday before his experience of Easter. The essential resurrection is one that brings us eternal life and love and happiness. Lazarus was brought back from the dead to temporary life in this world. He would die again, much as a critically ill person is saved on an operating table, thus purchasing several more years of life, but eventually dying of another cause.

Our Resurrection to Life Before We Die

However there is a deeper truth at stake here. Jesus told Martha he was the resurrection *and the life*. The image of resurrection makes us think of our bodies coming alive again in the future life, as we say in the creed, "I believe in the resurrection of the body." And that is a true teaching. But there is also "the life." This life is divine life, divine Love. It is eternal life, absolutely ebullient with Love.

"The life" is the life we have after we die and live with God, even though our bodies have not yet risen. But, more to the point, that is the life and love we have even now before we die. In baptism,

---

[*]Brown, Raymond, *The Gospel According to John*, Vol. 1 (Garden City, NY: Doubleday, 1966), p. 421.

the Eucharist, and the other sacraments we are initiated into the life of the resurrection — eternal life, divine life, everlasting Love. We do not need to wait until we die to "rise from the dead." What Jesus is saying is that resurrection from the death of the soul due to sin is his major gift to us. That resurrection is needed here even before we die.

All the miracles in John point to resurrection life here in this world as the necessary prelude to enjoying it in the next world. The wine miracle at Cana and the bread miracle on the mountain speak of the Eucharist that gives us risen life now. The cure of the official's son, the healing of the man at the pool of Bethesda are symbols of the new life we need for our souls. The resurrection of Lazarus is the most dramatic of the miracles that speak of Jesus as our resurrection — and our life.

This life is the theme that ties together Christ's dialogue with Nicodemus, his conversation with the Samaritan woman, his discourse on the Bread of Life. It is the central point of his declaration about his being the Living Water and the Light of the World at Tabernacles. His farewell discourse at the Last Supper will explore this teaching even more expansively.

For the Sake of the Nation
This Jesus Must Die (Jn. 11:45-57)

Jesus has just given life. The Sanhedrin met and concluded that he must die. Caiphas said, "It is better for you that one man should die instead of the people" (verse 50). The Passover will soon begin. Christ's enemies want to crush him completely. "This Jesus must die!" is the cry of his enemies. A miracle of life is cited as the last straw in demanding his death.

Reflection

1. What examples of the denial of death can I report from my experience?
2. Why do the some of the self-help books pay little attention to death and tragedy when they promise happiness?
3. Why does Jesus delay going to Bethany when he heard of the serious illness of Lazarus?

4. What is so remarkable about the faith confession of Martha in response to Jesus' words about resurrection?
5. How does Christ's reaction to the death of Lazarus affect me — "He trembled with deep emotion." "He shuddered, moved with deepest emotion?"
6. What are some of the funeral customs of Christ's time? How would they apply today?
7. When Thomas said, "Let us go and die with him," what does that say to me?
8. This resurrection story applies to the resurrection of my own body?It also speaks to resurrected life here. How?
9. In what way do I have eternal life and divine love before I die?
10. A miracle of life led the Sanhedrin to say, "This Jesus must die." What causes such blindness?

Prayer

Jesus, my resurrection, my life, I thank you for the gift of resurrected life even here before I die. I also look forward in faith to the resurrection of my body as I confess in the creed. Help me to grow in the divine grace of resurrected life and love here through the sacraments and spiritual development. Be my life. Be my love.

12 Oil for the Burial — Palms for the Messiah

Bethany: The Sweet Home of Love (Jn. 12:1-11)

Six days before his final Passover, Jesus went to Bethany to the home of Martha, Mary, and Lazarus. Pilgrims had already jammed the holy city of Jerusalem. Overflow crowds stayed at suburban villages such as Bethany. Martha cooked a festive meal. Family and friends celebrated the resurrection of their beloved Lazarus. Love had conquered death. Jesus, the embodiment of absolute love, reclined at table next to a man risen from the dead.

In the middle of the songs, stories, memories, and toasts of that glorious meal, Mary knelt before Jesus, took a pound of expensive perfume and anointed his feet, exuberantly giving him all the contents of the alabaster container. The perfume was spikenard, a sweet oil extracted from a plant in the Himalayas and imported from India. She unbound her hair and used it to dry his feet.

Martha had been the principal figure in the account of the resurrection of Lazarus. She left her home and went out to meet Jesus. Her dialogue of faith with him was the central commentary on the event about to happen. Her confession of faith concluded the narrative. John's gospel presents the typical Martha, extroverted, action oriented, slightly argumentative, loving, serving — and uncontestably a woman of profound faith.

Mary is the central person in the Bethany meal. Silence contains her. No words. No dramatic dialogues. No protests or arguments. This silent woman let her body do the talking. Kneeling in front of Jesus, she used up a bottle of perfume to anoint his feet. Then she dried them with her hair. Period. Let others do the talking, which they did.

Mary illustrated the nature of love's generosity and total self giving to another. Love does not worry much about the cost of a gift to the beloved. The gift must symbolize the total surrender of true love, regardless of the price which may be big or small. If the price is small, but that is all one has, that is total giving. Mary focused her loving attention completely on Jesus. Her deed was simplicity itself, humble, direct, uncomplicated, selfless, loving.

The powerful sweetness of the perfume filled the whole house. In telling this story, Mark and Matthew state that the fame of Mary's action would spread to the whole church. The Fathers of the church taught that the impact of her love for Jesus would fill the church.

Judas missed the loving purpose of Mary's deed and complained that she had just wasted enough money to pay a worker's wages for one year. Sounding smug, practical, even conscientious about the plight of the poor, Judas spoiled the festive tone of the celebration. He wielded guilt just when everyone was captivated by love. This charmless man stomped on the genial feelings of the community and insisted they have more concern for the poor.

His grumpy scolding of that cheerful group was confusing and unsettling. This was no self centered, heartless gathering of greedy people. These were people who believed in helping others and being concerned for the poor. Instinctively, they would never have seen a contradiction between the pure act of love they just saw and their moral obligations to the needy. They could easily have said, as Irish country people do, here is a man who came from a home that never bred a dream. Love and justice are friends not enemies.

In principle they did not deny they needed encouraging reminders to help the poor, but the timing was off. Jesus took their unspoken judgement and gave it words. He said to Judas, "Leave her alone. . . . You always have the poor with you, but you do not always have me" (verse 8). Mysteriously, he noted that Mary had anointed him for his burial. This was a time for loving him before he dies.

We should love and serve the poor at all times. We should also be alert enough to love people who are near and dear to us while we still have the time. At every graveside people say, "I wish I had done more. I regret I did not take time. It is too late now to do what I could have done when that person was still alive." Jesus was saying that they still had him in their midst. They could not have guessed that a week later he would be in the grave.

Jesus understood Judas better than the rest of them. The others were unaware of the fatal character flaw in the man. Jesus could size up people very well. Given his perceptive ability and the close quarters in which he lived with Judas over several years, he could tell that Judas was a troubled man.

Judas loved money too much. As a skilled money manager, he husbanded the resources of the small apostolic community, but his talent was also his devil. He never grasped the spiritual nature of their mission and failed completely to appreciate who Jesus was and what he hoped to do. Within the week, he would sell Jesus for money and betray his trust. Jesus tried to save him right up to the end, but Judas would not yield to love and salvation.

Jesus restored the good humor to their little dinner party. The squall passed, though his words about being anointed for his burial left a small cloud of unease. They would know soon enough what he meant. As the camera of our minds withdraws from that friendly scene, the light of the sunset puts all the guests in shadow, framing only two bodies reclining at table: Lazarus freshly risen from the dead and Jesus, destined to be buried a week later. Like shadowy angels, Mary and Martha stand as sentinels. Real angels would take their place at Easter.

Palm Sunday: If Tongues Were Silent, the Rocks Would Sing (Jn. 12:12-19)

The next day, Sunday, Jesus mounted an ass and rode into Jerusalem. Crowds came forth from the city. Waving palm branches, they shouted, "Hosanna! Blessed is he who comes in the name of the Lord, the king of Israel" (verse 13). They treated him as a rising political star who would rescue them from the control of the Roman government. They missed the significance of his choice of transportation, an ass, the sign of humility. The prophet Zechariah had pictured just such a scene of the messiah of peace and salvation coming to his people riding on a donkey (Zec. 9:9).

Freely, Jesus proceeded toward his holy passion to consummate the mystery of our salvation. The Word had come down from heaven to raise us from the depths of sin. He marched to his destiny without flags and banners, without knives and swords, without a retinue of threatening followers, without the symbols of power people like to use to put others in awe and submission. Meekly, humbly, simply he rode an awkward animal to the site of his blessed passion. The deluded crowds supplied the pomp, the banners of palms, the shouts of glory. In their minds they hailed a political liberator. But today, we use their acclamations in every Eucharist. We give those words their true meaning by acclaiming Jesus as a spiritual savior.

Quietly Jesus had entered the dark environment of our fallen world. The Word rejoiced that he could be humble for our sakes, become human and raise us up to a divine destiny. Christ's love for us never rested while he was on earth. Nor will his love cease in heaven where he strives to elevate our humanity to glory with him in heaven. On Palm Sunday he was not interested in the superficial glory heaped on him from other people. His only concern was to introduce them and us into the real glory — a union of absolute love and happiness with God. Human popularity is fickle. Divine popularity is eternal.

In our Christian imagination we can stand along the two mile road from Bethany to Jerusalem and see Jesus humbly riding an ass on his way to his holy passion. We see the people throwing their cloaks on the ground and waving palms. There is a certain thrill to it all, but also a dead end, a void. In a few hours the palms will wither. The songs of triumph will evaporate into the air and fall silent. People will hastily retrieve their cloaks and wrap them tightly around themselves to fend off the evening chill.

Jesus has given us something more substantial. He has cloaked us with baptism, the clothing of our salvation. In the imagery of the Bible, he has washed away the red stains of our sins and made us pure as white wool. He was not interested in being the conqueror of Rome, but the victor over sin and death. He has endowed us with that hope of victory. The very presence of our redeemed persons along the road of the march to the passion is our true palm branch. We — not the mere branches of a tree — are the palms he wants to see.

God so loved the world that he gave us Jesus. John's Palm Sunday narrative closes with prophetic words on the lips of the Pharisees, "Look, the whole world has gone after him" (verse 19).

The Greeks Wish to See Jesus (Jn. 12:20-36)

The religious leaders had fretted that the "whole world" was rallying to the side of Jesus. The first evidence of their comment was the appearance of some Greeks who came to Philip and asked him,

"Sir, we would like to see Jesus" (verse 21). The prophets had foreseen that the messiah would be the light of all peoples. The temple area had a section reserved for non-Jews. It was the Court of the Gentiles. Most likely it was there that visiting Greeks approached Philip and made their earnest request. Christ's enemies wanted to kill him. The Greeks wanted to visit with him.

In Luke's gospel, the Magi, the wise men from the east came to his birthplace at Bethlehem. In John's gospel the Greeks, the wisdom seekers from the west came to his deathplace in Jerusalem. The Magi beheld the Word in the form of a baby. The Greeks were to see the Word in the form of a criminal. Divine Providence had given the Magi the sign of a star to guide them to Christ. Jesus gave the Greeks the sign of a grain of wheat that must die in order to become the sheaf of wheat.

Wisdom seekers today want the reason for everything. They look for logic to solve the mysteries of life. The Greeks in this gospel looked for a person. Only the total embodiment of mystery is able to reveal the role of mystery in life. They wanted to experience a person, not just hear the musings of a disembodied brain. They did not seek a reason for everything. They sought an encounter with a person, Jesus, who would honor the hunger of their hearts with two splendid insights into the ultimate mystery he had come to witness.

Jesus shared two wisdom sayings with the wise men from the west. This was the beginning of the evangelization of nations. He modeled what he would tell his apostles and all of us to do. Preach and witness the Gospel of salvation.

One saying concerned the agricultural mystery of a seed and the process whereby it flowers. He did more than give the Greeks a lesson in biology which can only record the visible changes, but never uncover the final mystery of death and life. A seed must be buried in the earth, die and then rise to life as a sheaf of wheat. Jesus then applied the image to persons. "Whoever loves his life loses it, and whoever hates his life in this world will preserve it for eternal life" (verse 25). The humble agricultural mystery is a symbol of the noble mystery of human destiny. Death need not be thought of as the cancellation of all possibilities, but in fact the very road to the greatest possibility of all, total love in an everlasting life with God. Christ's redemptive death would make that possible.

God authored the book of nature that we might read about him in the wonders of creation. Hence the image of the grain of wheat. God also inspired the writing of revelation that we might read about him in the sacred Scriptures. Hence Christ's other wisdom saying, which was a stirring announcement of his passion. "The hour has come for the Son of Man to be glorified" (verse 23). Jesus used the word "hour" in a special manner. He did not refer to clock time, but to appropriate time. He was always thinking of his *return to his Father* through the cross, resurrection and ascension into heaven.

At Cana, Jesus had told Mary that this hour had not yet come. He was secure and safe throughout his Galilean ministry because his hour had not yet come. Now the hour has arrived. The prologue of this gospel stated that witnesses had seen the glory of the Word, experienced the glorious presence of divine Love. Where was this glory most strikingly seen? At the cross, when Jesus was lifted up to glory. That insight inspires the words of the hymn, "When I survey the wondrous cross, on which the Prince of Glory died." Small wonder that the cross is the central image of Christianity.

The Fathers of the church brought the intensity of their faith to the scene of the cross. They interpreted the last sacred breath of Jesus as the first breath of the Spirit he would send. The text lent itself to this understanding: "And bowing his head, he handed over the spirit" (Jn. 19:30). They observed with reverence the water and blood from his pierced side and wrote of them symbolizing baptism and the Eucharist. They were deeply moved by the testimony of faith from the soldier. "Truly, this man was the Son of God" (Mk. 15:39). The centurion had seen his glory even at the cross. And so have countless millions ever since.

John does not record the reaction of the Greeks. That will be given later by the Greek speaking peoples in Corinth, Athens, Ephesus, Crete, and many other places evangelized by the apostolic missionaries. "Gentiles" everywhere will come to faith in Jesus, the light of nations.

The prospect of death, however, was not going to be any easier for Jesus than for the rest of us. His glory language did not obscure his natural resistance to death or the pain and humiliation that would attend it. He must not only conquer death, but also his survival instincts that abhor the possibility of dying. He seemed to experience a mood change and it was the shadow of death that caused it. "I am troubled now. Yet what should I say? 'Father, save me from this hour'?" (verse 27). This was the kind of language he used in Gethsemane, a scene not described in John.

Just as at Gethsemane where he surrendered to his Father's will, so here in John he overcame the troubling prospect of death. He declared that it was for this purpose he had come, and he asked the Father to glorify his name. The listeners thought they heard thunder at that point when the Father's voice said from heaven, "I have glorified it and will glorify it again" (verse 28). In the Gethsemane narrative, an angel came and comforted him. In John, the Father gives his Son that blessed assurance.

Faith and Unbelief (Jn. 12:37-50)

This passage concludes the first half of the gospel, a section some call the Book of Signs, the chronicle of those miracles intended to open people to the glory-presence of God and call them to faith in Christ. Many refused to believe in Jesus. Others had begun to believe, but human respect and fear prevented them from professing their faith openly. The seed of their faith would only grow after it was watered by the blood of Christ. Two of these men were Nicodemus and Joseph of Arimathea, whom we will meet again after the crucifixion.

Next begins the Book of Glory, the narrative of the greatest of all Christ's signs — the sign of the cross.

Reflection

1. If Martha is the busy lady of the gospels, how was she able to exhibit such profound faith, as seen in the Lazarus story?
2. What lesson do I learn from the silent behavior of Mary in anointing Jesus?
3. What was basically wrong with the complaint of Judas at the Bethany dinner party?
4. How do I handle character flaws I see in those close to me?
5. Why did Jesus choose a donkey on which to ride into Jerusalem on Palm Sunday?
6. What "palms" should I wave before Jesus?

7. What are some similarities between the Greeks who wanted to see Jesus and the Magi who wanted to visit him?
8. Why did Jesus use such mysterious wisdom sayings when addressing the Greeks?
9. How can I become the "grain of wheat" in my Christian life?
10. How could the cross be a sign of Christ's glory?

Prayer

Jesus, friend of Martha, Mary, and Lazarus, you show me you have a need of close friends and brought to them the pleasure of your companionship. Help me to make my family a community of friendships and a center of hospitality. Let me welcome the "Greeks" — the people who need Christian love and service. I will become for them the "grain of wheat" to give them the bread of hope and comfort. I will show them the greatest glory, your cross and my life in union with it.

13   The Humble Commander — the Proud Disciple

The Foot Washing — Deep Reserves of Humility (Jn. 13:1-20)

The houses of Christ's time were usually one-storey buildings. Sometimes a room was built on the roof of the house. An outdoor stairway led up to it. This "Upper Room" was often used for storage, but sometimes it served as a conference room for a rabbi and his followers. It was in a room such as this that Jesus and his apostles gathered for the Last Supper.

Normally, no one entered a house without first taking off one's sandals and having one's feet washed. Dust and mud were removed from people's feet and the house was spared the dirt which might have been tracked in. Servants washed the feet of their employers. Poorer people washed one another's feet. We still have dust mats at doors and rugs in vestibules. Parents still train their children with the perennial words, "Wipe your shoes before coming in the house."

John writes that *while the meal was in progress* Jesus rose and took a towel and a basin of water and washed his apostles' feet. The customary washing outside the door of the Upper Room did not take place. Why not? Commentator William Barclay suggests that the argument among the apostles about who was the greatest among them was the reason (see Lk. 22:24). This petty rivalry on their way to the Last Supper would have stirred up their pride at the door to the Upper Room. Not one apostle would be willing to bend to another. After all the "greatest" expects a lesser person to do the dirty work.

Ever the Master Teacher, Jesus used this silly quarrel as a chance to teach them a lesson in true greatness. He had always loved his chosen disciples — warts and all — and he loved them to the very end. Disciples normally washed their master's feet as a sign of affection for their teacher. The grouchy mood generated by their competitive sparring caused them to forget this courtesy to Jesus — and prevented them from yielding an inch to one another.

Jesus proceeded to kneel before each one of them and wash their feet. The master cleansed his disciples' feet out of affection for them and to show them the source of real greatness. Six nights before, Mary of Bethany had anointed his feet with the sweet fragrance of love. On this holy Thursday night, Jesus washed his apostles' feet with the fresh water of humility and affection. Jesus witnessed the principle that really great people are truly humble.

The Resistance of Peter

When Jesus knelt before Peter, he looked up at a stubborn face. Peter held his feet back and told Jesus that he would never let him do such a humiliating task for him. At Caesarea Philippi, Peter had protested that he would never allow Jesus to undergo the humiliation of a public execution. He liked using the word "never."

Peter did not want a humble leader. He insisted on a dominant, forceful, overwhelming, proud, controlling-type leader. He envisioned a leader who pushed others around, not one who performed humble tasks. He clearly did not want a master who was willing to perform an act that even Jewish slaves were not required to do.

It was quite a scene. Jesus was in the submissive position. Peter, in the dominant pose. Yet the real authority was in the man who assumed a humble posture. His body talk was a prelude to the deeper emptying of the passion. The emptying of the divine glory by the Word become flesh had now bored more deeply into the human condition than ever before. Jesus had dug a new well into his immense resources to illustrate both the possibilities of human greatness as well as the extent to which divine Love was willing to go.

There is something helpless-looking about a man kneeling on the floor before another man. Nothing commanding about it. Beseechers look weak. Yet Jesus was totally at ease in a posture that appeared so vulnerable. The commander did not mind being humble. It was the proud soldier, Peter, who felt uncomfortable.

Patiently, almost like talking to a child, Jesus explained to Peter why he needed this humble attention: "Unless I wash you, you will have no inheritance with me" (verse 8). At Caesarea Philippi Jesus had harshly called Peter a "Satan" for tempting him to avoid his passion. In the soft glow of candlelight, Jesus was gentler with his intended chief of apostles, but no less severe in his challenge to faith. Whether he spoke with a rush of anger or quietly from the silence of his rock hard purposes, Jesus required faith in either case. If Peter wanted to share in an unimaginable Love, he must allow himself to be washed.

What is at stake here is something beyond a Sunday School lesson in the merits of humble greatness. Jesus was doing more than giving a good example of an attractive virtue. He was addressing the question of powerful personal change which could only be accomplished by his transforming Love and redemption. By his blood he would wash people from their sins. By this washing on Holy Thursday night he symbolized what he would do historically the next day. He demanded from Peter and all the apostles that they begin to accept his redemption with faith and trust.

The church Fathers were struck by the visual details John recorded in this scene and saw in each aspect the story of the Incarnation and Redemption (see verses 4-5). The Last Supper was like the heavenly banquet where the Word communed in love with the Father. The Word rose from it and laid aside the garment of glory and wrapped around himself the "towel" of humanity. He poured into the basin the regenerative waters of baptism and washed the apostles from their sins. Applying the drying towel, he dressed them with the "white robe" of risen life.

This is why some Christians have seen this ritual as a symbol of the baptismal rite. Foot washing was a ceremony that admitted one into the sanctity of one's home. Baptism is the sacramental ceremony that welcomes one into the household of the faith.

To return to the scene at hand: Jesus had once told Nicodemus that no one can enter the kingdom of God without being born again of water and the Holy Spirit. Now to Peter he said basically the same thing. Peter could not enter the community of Love — be part of Jesus' Kingdom — without being washed in water and the Word.

Jesus gave Peter some time for reflective silence. As Peter faced this call to faith, there may possibly have been a procession of lepers going by the house. If so he would hear the ringing of their bells and their sad cry — "Unclean!" — which they were required to call out by local law and custom. That would have been an occasion for insight into his own spiritual need for cleansing. When he was finally moved to speak, he burst out with his usual impetuous bent, "Master, then not only my feet, but my hands and head as well" (verse 9).

Jesus may have smiled at the excessive mood swings of his beloved Peter. He told this loveable man that the footwashing would be enough. Then Jesus completed his ceremony. They were all washed with water by the Word. Symbolically, this ceremony not only called them to faith in the kingdom but also to be evangelizers on behalf of the kingdom. Those washed feet should go out and bear the Gospel to the whole world. Years before, Isaiah had put the image to poetry. "How beautiful upon the mountains are the feet of him who brings glad tidings . . . bearing good news, announcing salvation" (Is. 52:7).

At the completion of this ceremony, Jesus told them to do exactly what he did. They should practice the greatness of humility and wash people in the waters of salvation. Humility is the attitude. Evangelizing performance is the behavioral expectation.

In this age of fretting over one's self worth, it may seem too much to ask to try humility. In a sense this is true. One cannot humble a self that has not yet been properly discovered. Self worth is acquired by being open to the love others wish to confer on us. Some may need to make a *psychological act of faith* in the need to change to obtain the first step in self esteem.

But there is another necessary step and that is a *religious act of faith* in Jesus whose love will permeate us with the most stable form of self esteem, one based on identity with the image of God, which is a divine gift to all people. The third step in this process is a humble losing of self in order to find the truest self of all, the redeemed self, cleansed of sin and filled with grace.

At this point we are ready to evangelize because our hearts have been fused with divine Love. What else shall Love in our hearts do but rise to our lips, quicken our feet and urge all the world to come to Christ.

The Traitor at the Meal of Love (Jn. 13:21-30)

For most of us the experience of betrayal will anger us. Betrayal is a razor that draws blood. Jesus knew that Judas had treasonous intentions. Jesus could have withered him like the fig tree, or torn him apart as his death would do to the veil of the temple. But the gospels report no such violent impulses in Jesus toward Judas. At the same time, John reports that Judas deeply "troubled" Jesus.

St. Augustine was intrigued by this recorded feeling of Jesus, who had "power" to lay down his life and raise it up again. Judas troubled the mighty power of Jesus and appeared to disturb the firmness of the rock. Augustine suggests that it is our weakness that is troubled in Jesus. Our Lord, who would die for us, was troubled in our place. He died in power, yet was troubled in the midst of that power. He would transform our humble bodies into bodies of glory — similar to his. Just so, he assumed into himself the experience of our weakness and sympathized with us in the feelings of his own soul.

But such feeling never caused him to fail. He remained the courageous, sure, unconquerable savior. He was not faltering in his purpose or in danger of perishing, but as the Good Shepherd he was reaching out to us who might slip and perish. It is in beholding his troubled spirit that we survive our own anxieties and avoid hopelessness. By consenting freely to experience that troubling experience caused by Judas, he consoles us who often must bear our own troubles unwillingly. In a word, he gives us hope.

Jesus said to his apostles, "One of you will betray me" (verse 21). His statement caused a small sensation in that little dinner gathering. Each man there knew what his own conscience told him. Each self assured apostle looked with suspicion at the others around the table. Peter acted to dispel this uncertainty. He nodded to John, "the disciple whom Jesus loved," to ask Jesus who was the traitor. John reclined next to Jesus and leaned back against Christ's heart and asked the identity of the man. John rested against Christ's secret source of wisdom, his heart, and sought the source of this tragedy.

Jesus had no intention of exposing Judas to the tender mercies of a suddenly angered apostolic band. He would never want his final meal to turn into a brawl. His purposes were always directed at saving every person, Judas included. His words to John about it being the man to whom he next gave a morsel of food did not seem to settle the question for the disciples did not conclude that Judas was the man. Christ seemed to act and speak in a deliberately ambiguous way in their eyes.

John reclined on Christ's right, hence his head would be near Christ's heart. But Judas was on Christ's left, so that the head of Jesus was near the heart of Judas. Jesus dipped some bread in a dish of moist herbs and offered it to Judas. As soon as that apostle took it, Satan entered him. His decision to betray was finalized at that moment. Jesus wanted Judas to reconsider. Offering him the bread of friendship was a gesture that said, "I want to give you love. Believe in my affection for you."

Judas had closed his heart to Jesus and Satan moved in. Jesus recognized that surge of evil presence. He would not force the will of Judas, so he permitted him to pursue his treacherous goal. "What you are going to do, do quickly" (verse 27). Even that order to leave the dinner did not alarm the other apostles. It was customary to give a gift of money or food to a poor person as part of the Passover celebration. The apostles easily could have assumed that Judas, the treasurer, was despatched on this errand of charity.

This episode at the supper closes with the vivid comment:
"And it was night" (verse 30).

Christ's Command to Love (Jn. 13:31-35)

Then Jesus established the theme of his Last Supper with them, a principle that was central to his whole mission. "I give you a new commandment: love one another. As I have loved you, so you also should love one another" (verse 34).

What is new about this commandment? Was this not already commanded in the ancient law of God? "You shall love your neighbor as yourself" (Lv. 19:18). Why is it called new, when it is obviously so old? The new element is found in Christ's addition, "as I have loved you." This distinguishes his view of love from all the kinds found on earth. When Jesus loved people he did so that they might be brought to God. Christ's love awakened the awareness of the divine presence in people. His love led people to accept God into their lives.

He was like a good doctor who loves his patients. The doctor does not love the sickness, but the health he wants to bring his ailing people. He removes the sickness and brings forth one's health. Jesus approaches us as spiritual patients whose sinfulness must be removed and in whom the health and wholeness of God is placed.

Christ's love always has a divine purpose. If we are to love as Christ did, then we should love in such a way that God comes into the lives of those we meet.

"This is how all will know that you are my disciples, if you have love for one another" (verse 35). Christians have much in common with all peoples — intelligence, language, beauty, bravery, humanitarian impulses, energy, religious rituals, family life, patriotic commitments, etc. The question is, what makes a Christian different? That they are lovers? That they love each other? Do not other people love?

The mark of Christian disciples is that they have faith in Jesus and love as Jesus did, a love that joyfully opens the beloved to the experience of God, a love that saves people from sinfulness by the grace of Christ. Christian love is always an evangelizing love. Because this evangelizing is done in love, the other person's freedom is reverenced. The Christian loves with the humility of a Jesus who kneels before the human race — as he did at the foot washing — and offers the gift of cleansing from evil's slavery. Christian love never forgets the mission of the world's salvation. For the Christian disciple, love without God's salvation is unthinkable. It is the most powerful of all the kinds of love on the planet earth.

A Rooster and Tears for Peter (Jn. 13:36-38)

Peter sensed that Jesus was headed for danger. He wanted to be with him to protect him. Jesus told him that he could not follow him at this time. In the future that will be possible. Peter argued that he was quite prepared to follow him into the worst danger, even to die to save him. Jesus answered, "Will you lay down your life for me? Amen, amen, I say to you, the cock will not crow before you deny me three times" (verse 38).

Peter had insufficient insight into himself. He overestimated his strength. His desires outstripped his abilities. Peter promised to die for Jesus, before Jesus died for Peter. He would need more than the blustery courage based on physical strength and a romantic idealism that was not really spiritual. He needed spiritual power, the kind that would come from the redemptive act of Jesus. The presumption of courage without a spiritual base would not work.

It was probably not without pain that Jesus told him that before dawn — before a rooster crowed three times — Peter would deny him three times. Jesus would not have enjoyed telling Peter the unpleasant truth about himself. But it was a truth that he hoped would make Peter free to be spiritually courageous. It did not work. Peter would indeed deny his Lord.

Only after the sin of his denial did his true spiritual conversion begin. After his third denial and the third crow of the cock, he saw Jesus emerge from the High Priest's house. He saw Jesus look at him with kindness and love — the Love that introduces a saving God into the house of one's soul. Then he was touched so deeply that he went out and wept tears of repentance and change. He died to the old Peter in his denial. He rose to the new Peter in his tears.

Many of us will see ourselves in Peter's story. We try to achieve spiritual goals with non-spiritual means. If we are fortunate we shall see the look of Christ's urging us to tears of repentance and conversion. Then we shall have our personal resurrection in him.

Reflection

1. Why was there a failure to have the footwashing at the door of the Upper Room at the Last Supper?
2. What was Peter's view of leadership? What is mine?
3. What kind of struggles have I had in trying to be humble?
4. How is the story of the foot washing connected with the Sacrament of Baptism?
5. If I have a poor sense of self esteem, how will I be able to be humble?
6. The intended betrayal by Judas troubled Jesus. How did St. Augustine reflect on this "troubling feeling" of Jesus?
7. What is so new about Christ's "new" commandment of love?
8. How much does Christ's view of love appear in my own loving behavior to others?
9. How can my relatives, friends, and acquaintances tell I am Christ's disciple?
10. What are incidents in my life that are reflected in the story of Peter's denial?

Prayer

Eucharistic Lord, your Last Supper was marred by the betrayal of Judas into whose soul Satan entered and by the prophecy of Peter's denial. I am thus reminded that in the most sacred and loving situations, the jarring remnants of sinfulness abide. Purify me from all tendencies to betray or deny you. Fill me with the love you described in your New Commandment, a love that brings a saving God into the lives of all people I touch.

14   The Great Sermon at the Lord's Supper

Chapters 14-17 of this gospel contain the "Last Supper Discourse." John did not include the words of the institution of the Eucharist in his account of the Last Supper, as was seen in all the synoptic gospels. We pointed out that he gave Christ's teaching about the Eucharist in his Bread of Life dialogue in chapter 6. Here John gives us Christ's profound reflection on his relationship to his Father and the Spirit. Around the table of fellowship, where Jesus celebrated his last Passover with his closest friends, he invited them to share in his relationship with his Father and the Spirit. That was the ultimate meaning of their Communion with him in his Body and Blood. His words to them are his words to us. The Great Sermon at the Last Supper was meant to be written on our hearts.

We Do Not Know the Way . . .
Show Us Your Father (Jn. 14:1-14)

Jesus knew that within the next twenty-four hours he would be dead. His apostles still did not suspect this. People who know they are about to die will sum up a lifetime's worth of wisdom to pass on to their families and friends. Christ's Great Sermon at the Last Supper was delivered in this spirit.

He began his remarks with words about leaving. He tried to relieve their fears and anxieties about losing him forever. He asked them to trust him, no matter what happened. They must believe that he was leaving them to prepare a heavenly life for them. He would return and take them to himself. He reminded them that he had many times described for them the Way to this new Love and Life.

But did they know the Way?

Thomas spoke for them all by claiming they did not.

"Master . . . how can we know the way?" (verse 5).

Christ's witness, teachings, and miracles had not yet penetrated the hearts and minds of these eleven men who had been given the most extraordinary spiritual seminar in history. For three years, by means of one-on-one personal encounter, as well as public sermons, dialogues, miracles, debates, dinner conversations, long talks on hikes, responses to problems and questions, the impressive example of his behavior, the powerful pull of his personality, and every other imaginable effort to reach them, Jesus had still only touched the surface of their souls.

This difficulty Jesus had with them would become even clearer in a moment when Philip would make a remark similar to that of Thomas. It will take the sign of glory — the sign of the cross — to open them up and rip apart the veil of their dull comprehensions. Even after that, it will require the continuing presence and power of the Holy Spirit to make this possible.

The process of Christian transformation is not a simple matter even when the best of all spiritual directors is available. That is as true for us as it was for our good friends at the Last Supper.

Jesus replied, "I am the way and the truth and the life" (verse 6).

The way is the way of the cross.

The truth is the fidelity Jesus witnessed to every person as well as the truths of his message that makes us free.

The life is love, the love that comes as a gift from the sanctuary of the Trinity.

The Way

The first name for Christianity was "The Way." It implied both the life of moral virtues which Christians tried to witness and above all their commitment to discipleship. This meant revealing the glory-presence of God through living the sign of the cross. Lose the self. Take the cross. Follow Jesus. We Christians will always struggle with this Way. We will try to find substitutes. We will prefer a softer religion. We will want only Easter and not Good Friday. We will seek a pretty religion, not the blood, dirt, pain, and evil smells of death that come with the cross.

Jesus made it clear that the Way would never be easy. He first walked that Way himself to show us how to do it. He did not promise us a rose garden without thorns. To imagine the Way without suffering is to corrupt Christianity. But to be lifted up on our cross is to be lifted up to glory, to be flooded with divine light and be transformed into a lifestyle that will provide us with the most extraordinary possibilities for happiness.

The Truth

Throughout his ministry Jesus insisted that his message was true. He spoke truths. He was not voicing opinions that could be disputed and proven to be inferior to other opinions. Jesus was not a relativist in the marketplace of ideas. He claimed that what he said was absolutely true. His message of truths has survived two thousand years of efforts to disprove them and reduce them to mere opinions that float away with the next wind of fashion.

Today's climate of relativism (There is no truth, only opinions.) is nothing new. Century after century, one or another form of it has surfaced again and again, always hoping to dislodge the truths of Jesus from influencing people's intellectual and moral lives. It is these truths that have liberated the minds of Christians and opened them to the inner freedom that is such a precious gift.

Lies enslave. Truths liberate.

At the Last Supper Jesus went further. He told the apostles that he not only had the truth — he was the Truth. By this he meant that truth should be more than food for the intellect. It must also be the iron that tightens our ability to be faithful to God, others and self. Truth is also the food for commitment, loyalty, and fidelity. This above all to your own self be true, to your friend be true, to your God be true. And then you shall never be false to anyone. A truth in the mind that never affects behavior will wither. Truth only gives us inner freedom when we act on it. The most obvious outcome of truth in the mind is fidelity in our behavior.

This is the wholistic view of truth Jesus brought to full flower at the Great Supper. Our society needs his vision more than ever. It is no great surprise that once it taught relativism — that truth in the mind is impossible to find — then fidelity in behavior became a scarce commodity. Modern culture, therefore, has become a desert scattered with the bones of broken commitments. Jesus tells us he is Truth. He is a living example of fidelity. He kept his promises. This is the total vision of Truth, the one that will do much to heal broken families, fractured friendships, and all the other kinds of chaotic relationships in our contemporary world.

The Life

Lastly, Jesus is the Life.

Only where there is Love is there Life. Someone once put a sign on his desk, "Died at 45 — Retired at 65." People who have ceased to love drift into a living death. The pervasive unhappiness of many people is largely attributable to the slow dying that comes from the loss of the capacity to love and be loved. Love is more likely to die when it has ceased to be a love that brings God into one's relationships with others, God, and self. Jesus has already spoken of his new commandment of love, a saving love, a love that redeems one from all kinds of oppression, above all from sin.

Sin is death. Divine Love is Life. At the Lord's Supper, the apostles communed with the bread and wine become the Body and Blood of Christ. They had communed with Life, with visible Love. Eternal Life had entered their spiritual bloodstream. Jesus was now explaining to them what their experience meant.

The seemingly innocent question of Thomas about how to find the Way evoked from Jesus his remarkable revelation of himself as Way. . . Truth . . . Life. Another apostolic remark prepared for a further splendid revelation. Jesus said that no one could reach the Father except through him. Like the shepherd who laid his body across the opening to the sheepfold, Jesus was the gate to heaven and access to the Father. Philip was so excited by this that he enthusiastically said, "Show us the Father and that will be enough for us" (verse 8).

See Me — See Your Father

Sounding impatient, Jesus reminded Philip of all the months and years they have been together. In all this time, has not Philip understood what Jesus was doing and saying? (See above comment on the full range of teaching, example and personal contact Jesus used to open up his apostles to the power of personal change in mind, heart, feelings, soul, and body.). There is a tone of exasperation in Christ's reply. And yet this situation drew from him a line that remains to this day a point for boundless reflection:

"Whoever has seen me has seen the Father" (verse 9).

Familiarity with someone does not necessarily produce an insight into that person. How often we say, "I really never knew her" . . . "He was always a mystery to me." Valuable as it is, the experience of a person does not automatically reveal who that person really is. Even loving spouses at silver wedding anniversaries have been known to say, "We are just getting to know each other."

This is even more true in an age where we believe that observing the outer behavior of a person is the key to knowing the inner core of that man or woman. Surveys of personality traits, examinations of sexual attitudes, profiles of administrative talents, IQ tests, reports of spending habits, compatibility quotients, emotional stability, and political choices still leave most of us in the dark about the inner mystery of the human person.

Philip had plenty of evidence about Jesus. But what he saw with his eyes only gave him sight, not insight. He liked Jesus, even loved him. One would have thought this would have led him to really know him. Love songs say, "To love me is to know me." But poets reply that love is blind and tragically lovers do not see. Still, love songs and poets are talking about romance and the bubbly, superficial emotion of inexperienced and untested love. Sad as it may be to report, too many people are sluggish in their relating, even to their best friends. What passes for love is merely sloth for the partners in the relationship have made little effort to truly know one another.

Philip made Jesus painfully aware of how thin was the level of insight his apostles had in him. They had the benefit of superb instruction. They saw miracles performed with authority. They beheld actions that only a God could do — sins forgiven, secret thoughts revealed, death taking flight, eyesight created from the clay of the earth.

The most remarkable thing about Christ's reaction was that he gave them even a greater revelation to chew on. He did not take out the baby food and start over. Nor did he concede to their weakness and hint that, well, after all such a revelation is too much for people. If they did not think it was possible, then maybe it was not. Jesus rejected this approach. He did not fashion his teaching out of the mistakes and weaknesses of his listeners nor remake revelation to fit their dim perceptions.

Instead, Jesus let lightning strike the Upper Room. As good Jews they all knew that one would die if one saw God. Moses had to veil his face when talking to God. Even at the burning bush, he bowed his eyes to the ground and took off his shoes in fearful dread before the face of God. Firm voiced and deliberate, Jesus lifted his apostles to a new level of vision. They could look on nim and live. In fact, they could only live by looking at the glory he was revealing. To have spiritual insight into him is to know the Father.

He is not saying that he is the Father, but that he is the image of the Father. He and his Father are one. The Father who seemed to scare the prophets entered that Upper Room of affection and love in the middle of the most amiable moment of their liturgical year, the Passover. It has now become the celebration of the Eucharist, a friendship meal of sacrificial love. And the Father is there. Absolutely united to his Son. Jesus did not pat them on the heads with palliatives of watered-down teaching. He resolutely pushed them beyond their limited horizons.

Despite their blindness, he knew the peaks of faith of which they were capable and gloriously led them there. Stubbornly, he held their feet to the fire to mature them in belief. His affection was not the soft pastels of a greeting card, but the roaring and sumptuous primary colors of the sunrise. The Father was as available as the Jesus who sat before them.

Jesus Will Send the Holy Spirit (Jn. 14:14-31)

Jesus repeated again that he was leaving them. If they loved him they would keep his commandments, especially the "new commandment." He revealed to them that the Holy Spirit would become part of their lives. This Spirit would provide them with the same kind of intimate presence they had known in their relationships with him. The Spirit would bring back to their memories all he had said to them and open their hearts to the real meaning and possibilities of the Gospel.

In a sense he was telling them why they still did not appreciate who he was, what he said and what he taught. Until he was lifted up to glory on the cross and until the Spirit came, they would still flounder in their inadequate grasp of his ministry to them. The redemption would deliver them from their darkness and the coming of the Spirit would provide the insight so difficult for them to acquire up to this point. He did not want his impatience with Philip to frighten them. Nor should the passion cause them to lose hope. "Do not let your hearts be troubled or afraid" (verse 27).

Even if he flooded them with such ineffable revelations — insights presently beyond them — he let them know he understood their difficulties. He treated them as adults, but always with compassion for the problems they had in believing in him and his message. They may not be able to take it all in that evening in the Upper Room, but when the Spirit came they would be granted the gift of insight and the courage to act on it.

Never intending to leave them without hope, he spoke of giving them his peace, that sense of inner harmony wherein one is reconciled to self, others, and God. His peace was different from the world's peace which is more of a truce, an uneasy pause in life's confrontations. The world's peace is imposed by force. Christ's peace is offered in freedom. The world's peace requires security arrangements. Christ's peace creates inner security that liberates one from fear, sin, and death. This is experienced by us more clearly in the Sacrament of Reconciliation.

After Good Friday, Easter, the Ascension, and Pentecost the apostles will begin to assimilate the impact of these first words of the Last Supper Discourse. Jesus strove to allay their fears that night and share his inner peace with them. In the years to come his Holy Spirit will continue this work and much, much more.

Reflection

1. Why should Thomas have known what was the "Way" of which Jesus spoke?
2. When Jesus said he was the Way, what did he mean?
3. What is relativism? What examples of relativism do I see in life around me?
4. What are the two meanings of Jesus as Truth?
5. What is the connection between Truth and fidelity?
6. How do I understand Christ's words that he is the Life?

7. Why did Jesus sound slightly exasperated when Philip asked him, "Show us the Father"?
8. How would I explain Christ's words that to see him is to see the Father?
9. What events would make it more possible for the apostles to understand what Jesus was telling them that evening? Why were such events necessary?
10. In what two ways did Jesus try to console his apostles that evening?

Prayer

Lord Jesus, Way, Truth and Life, help me to walk the way of the cross. Send your Spirit to teach me your truth and to give me the courage to be faithful to God, others and myself. Train me in the saving Love that identifies me with your Life. May your Spirit also endow me with the insight to see the Father in you and you in the Father. Thank you for liberating me from fear and for giving me your reconciling peace.

15 The Bonfire of the Branches Without Jesus

Intimacy With Jesus Is Like a Vine and a Branch (Jn. 15:1-8)

Jesus loved to use the images of daily life to illustrate his Gospel. In this Last Supper discourse, his lesson drawn from grape farming is a case in point. Grape farmers planted their vines on terraced slopes above their grain fields. In those cooler highlands they could count on heavy dewfall even in the dry summer months. They planted the vines in rows about eight feet apart, giving them plenty of growing space as well as room for the workers to move through them.

Every spring the farmers pruned the vines. "When the flowering is ended, and the blooms are succeeded by ripening grapes, Then comes the cutting of the branches with pruning hooks and the discarding of the lopped-off shoots" (Is. 18:5). The workers walked through the rows, pausing at each vine to cut off the less productive branches with a small knife. They brought the piles of branches to a safe area where they were burned. The living branches that were heavy with prospective fruit were propped up with forked sticks. Lastly, the farmers gently loosened the ground around the vines with a hoe and scraped away any weeds. After that they waited while mother nature matured the small clusters of fruit which swelled and ripened under the hot summer sun. At harvest time the workers lived in makeshift shelters by the vineyards to guard them.

Participants at a Passover meal would have drunk four ceremonial cups of wine. At the Last Supper the third cup of wine was transformed sacramentally by Jesus into his Blood. The drinking of the Sacramental Wine would have been a perfect lead-in to his comments about the vine and the branches. Images of vines, grapes and wine were among the most pleasant in their minds since they spoke of fruitfulness, color, joyful celebration, and warm hearts.

Often they praised God for "producing bread from the earth, and wine to gladden men's hearts" (Ps. 104:15).

When Jesus began to talk about vine farming he induced a mellow mood that matched the progress of the meal and his words about peace as well as his attempts to keep them from being anxious or afraid. He would have prompted in their minds the many wine songs they had chanted, the laughter of the harvesters, the village dances that accompanied the festivals of the wine harvests. In their imaginations they would have seen again the bonfires at night where the pruned branches lit up the sky.

Jesus chose the image to illumine the mystery of his intimacy with them. They had just drunk of the sacred cup of sacramental wine — his precious Blood. The setting and their experience lent themselves perfectly to Christ's words: "I am the true vine and my Father is the vine grower" (verse 1). In response to Philip's request, Jesus had helped them to experience the presence and availability of the Father at that very meal. The Father is the vine grower and Jesus is the vine.

Jesus pressed the truth about his relationship to them in terms of intimacy. He and they were more than acquaintances. They were as close to each other as a vine is to a branch. The vine is the life-giver. The branch is the life-receiver. They had just drunk of his very Blood, another name for life. They must realize that their access to divine Life and Love is through Jesus. They may try to save themselves by using their own wits, intelligence, physical energy, political connections, family wealth, membership in the patriarchal religion, or a dozen other means. None of it will work. Only intimacy with Jesus will benefit them. "I am the vine, you are the branches" (verse 5).

As the life-giving juice of the vine pours into a branch causing a flower to bloom and a small fruit to appear, so does the transforming juice of Christ's love and grace pour into them to make them courageous, committed and productive disciples. "Without me, you can do nothing" (verse 5). If they withdraw from Jesus as a person, cease to listen to his word, and depart from communing with him in the Eucharist, they will become the fruitless branches that will be knifed off the vine and thrown onto a bonfire.

Every age tempts Christians to try some other way to find happiness and freedom without Jesus. In our own time some people withdraw from Eucharist for ideological reasons. Others prefer the writings of secular wisdom to the Gospel teachings of Jesus. Some teach that Jesus is not the only One by whom we shall be saved, despite the biblical teaching, "Nor is there any other name under heaven given to the human race by which we are to be saved" (Acts 4:12). Some write books and articles about Christianity, yet never even mention the name of Jesus, a name that means "Savior." These approaches will lead such people to become branches disconnected from the Vine that is Jesus Christ. Lacking intimacy with Jesus, they risk being cut off and thrown into the bonfire.

The bonfire is spiritual burnout in this life and hell in the next. The branches of our lives dry up in the desert without love. We may have sought vitality in the quest for money, sex and power, which gave us momentary relief from inner pain. We could have let the force which makes flowers grow and planets spin course through our lives. Through Jesus, the Word, all things were made. All reality lives, moves and has its being in him. The river of his creative force could stream through our lives. We may choose to be branches on his vine or go off on our own. Should we decide to walk alone, we will head for the bonfire.

Christian spirituality centers on Christ. He is the truth that we speak, the way we walk, the love we show to others. The agricultural symbol of the vine and branches refers to a psychological and spiritual relationship with Jesus. Branches and vines must stay together if there is to be a grape harvest. The image evokes the connections seen in all friendships and the pursuit of love. People who want to be friends must work on their friendships. Spouses who hope to stay together must stay in touch with each other.

We must work on our friendship with Christ if we expect to be effective Christians. The pledge to be Christ's friend, begun in baptism, must be a lifelong project. Someone has said, "If I don't mend my friendships and mind my love relationships, I shall soon be without friends or lovers." Neither love nor friendship can be taken for granted.

Friendship with Jesus is no different. We must think of him. We must try to be near him. We must allow the give and take that characterizes any relationship. Christ the vine and the Christian branch must stick together. The flow of life and love between branch and vine leads to the wine of Christian love that cheers the heart of God, others, and self.

The fast pace of today's life causes many people to forget the time needed to have a vital relationship which needs constant attention. Doing things for one another is not enough. Persons are more important than things. Merely being together will not suffice. Even branches still on the vine dry up and die. Physical presence is a start but more is needed. There must be intimacy between the persons, a sharing of oneself with the other, be that a spouse, a relative, a friend — or Jesus. The process is the same. So long as the flow of meaning, care and concern occurs, the relationship will be healthy and growth will happen.

There is a significant difference, however, when the relationship is between Jesus and us. The process is similar to those we have with spouses, relatives, and friends. But when our partner is Jesus the life-giver, the flow of vitality that comes from him to us is qualitatively superior to any love we would ever receive from anyone else.

When we relate to him, we touch the life-force itself. We encounter a creativity that makes us new, a forgiveness that clarifies our whole inner life, a dynamism that releases interior energies we never knew existed within us. We become pure, not just by the absence of the darkness of evil, but by the presence of a light that shows us how all our parts fit together in harmony. Our will. Our emotions. Our minds. Our bodies. Affected by his Love, our inner disorder gives way to a friendly union of all our faculties. This, too, takes time. But it is a process which no other love relationship can achieve. In Jesus, we become centers of peace for all those we meet.

You Are My Friends (Jn. 15:9-17)

In case the apostles do not appreciate the real meaning of the vine image, Jesus proceeded to talk about love. Jesus said the kind of love the Father has for him is the same kind he has for them — and us as well. He immediately connected love with obedience, a Gospel value that seems out of fashion today, but has always been a bit unfashionable even in the time of the apostles, not to mention the Garden of Eden. Christ mentioned love in the same breath as obedience to his commandments. Lest we think we are the only ones doing the obeying, he added that our obedience should be like his own obedience to his Father's commandments.

For a variety of reasons obedience has had a bad press in our times. Horror stories about the misuse of authority have given obedience a terrible name. The Nazi war trials gave us a spectacle of brutal murderers excusing their crimes under the guise of obedience. "I was simply following orders as I turned the gas on the women and children." Bruised adults today often attribute their wrecked psyches to abusive parents who forced them to obey, using terror and fear to obtain submission. Even religion has been misused when harsh authority extracted obedience for unworthy purposes. Worst of all has been the seventy-year record of Marxist-Communism which has enslaved the wills of millions of people and made them obey or else suffer death or imprisonment.

Nevertheless, even though obedience has been debased by such hateful usage, it remains a scriptural value. Just because various kinds of authority — parental, political, military, religious — have sometimes wrongfully imposed unjust obedience, does not excuse us from practicing true, Christian obedience. And it certainly does not justify the cult of disobedience. Such evil usage simply challenges us to rehabilitate obedience in the light of Christ's example and teachings. Jesus told the apostles that he obeyed his Father's commandments. Paul reminded the Philippians of just how deep was the obedience of Jesus. "He humbled himself, becoming obedient to death, even death on a cross" (Phil. 2:8).

Jesus established love as the context for his remark about obedience. The condition for scriptural obedience is love. "If" one loves, then one obeys. Love, however, is expected from both partners to the experience. Ideally, the commander should love the commanded. Conversely, the obeyer should love the commander. This is love in the form of trust, not fear. Between adults this exchange should take place in a perspective of equality, respect for the dignity of those engaged. When we have a case of lovers, this is no problem. Lovers easily say, "Your wish is my command." Obedience here is a joy, not a burden.

But when the exchange is between one who is officially "superior" to another, the interaction is trickier. The one who has "rank" should not view the obeyer as inferior in terms of humanity and personhood. Our world is full of bosses. Public administration in all its forms can probably happen in no other way. But the bosses should not be bossy. And they certainly should not oppress, intimidate, and humiliate those responsible to them in order to enforce obedience. At the same time, the obeyers should act responsibly, with trust and respect and openness.

Obviously, this is a complex topic and we cannot explore the full variety of commander-obeyer relationships and how to do it best. All we wish to insist on is that life requires a proper form of authority and a suitable response of obedience. Jesus situated his "obedience" talk in the context of love and friendship. He promised his apostles that he would love them in the greatest way he knew how. He would lay down his life for them, just as a shepherd risks his life for his flock.

He had no intention of treating them as inferiors. "I have called you friends" (verse 15). He loved them and treated them as his loved ones. He chose them. He did not pick them because they were good. His choice elevated them to a goodness they had not known before. He did not love them because they were so loveable. It was his love that made them loveable.

In religious language this is the mystery of grace. God finds us as sinners, basically unlovable, prone to evil, lost, mired in our own darknesses. His grace touches us and turns us into his beloved. In child talk, the frog becomes a prince, the ugly duckling becomes a swan. We have the potential to undergo this remarkable transformation from slaves of sin to friends of God. Divine Love makes us loveable.

Return then to the subject of obedience. Its root meaning comes from the Latin "to hear and respond." When Jesus says to us, "I choose you to be a friend," we have the option to say yes or no. When we say "yes," we are obeying with love and trust. This is creative and redemptive obedience which opens us to being true, beautiful, loveable and one with God. Keeping Christ's commandments in this perspective only deepens the friendship which has begun.

On the Other Hand —
The World's Hatred for Christians (Jn. 15:18-27)

By this point the apostles could hardly have felt better about themselves. The glow of love had seized their hearts. Peace had settled the noise of their inner selves. The warmth of their celebratory meal had never made them feel so comfortable before. The Master had acknowledged clearly that they were deep friends of his. Fear had fled. Anxiety had subsided. Already a genial complacency had soothed them. They, the branches, felt a healthy flow of life from the vine, Jesus.

Ever the realist, Jesus decided they were strong enough now to receive a jolt. They suspected he was in some kind of danger. They did not realize that a lifetime of danger lay ahead of them. Jesus stripped them of any illusions about their future. The world would hate them and kill them and persecute them just as it planned to do to him. The friends of Jesus would suffer just as he did. Their love bond with him would include the cross. He would suffer and die tomorrow. They would suffer and die soon enough.

The cause was identical — the world that hates the Father, the world that hates the Son, the world that hates real Christians. The hatred arises from commitment to evil and sin. The world's hatred refuses to accept salvation from sin, because it does not want to give up evil. It prefers its own hatred to the possibility of divine love and redemption.

The center of the world's opposition is in its will, the core of choice. Since it will not make the option for love, it chooses hatred instead and wreaks its vengeance on those who have chosen Jesus and Love. Disobedience, refusal to hear and respond to Christ's invitation to a life of love and moral virtue is the world's choice. Because the friends of Jesus will witness to his person and message, they will suffer at the hands of those who hate God and prefer evil.

The Acts of the Apostles and the Book of Revelation amply prove that Jesus' words on that Holy Night would come true. Church history ever since has abundant testimony about the persecution of the friends of Jesus. The most powerful ideology of the twentieth century, Marxist Communism, was based upon a militant atheism that systematically tried to destroy the friends of Jesus.

In the free societies of the industrial nations there is a noticeable hostility to Christianity. Christians who defend the rights of the unborn are branded as an outcast fringe who must be co-opted and suppressed. Christians who question the sexual freedoms of the culture as destructive of family life are ridiculed. Christians who stand up for economic justice for the poor are sidetracked by the super-moneyed class. Christians who plead for peace are considered strange and even a threat. Christians who say that there is such a thing as truth are reviled by the relativists. Christians who assert that

God must have a place in civil law and culture are fought against as though it was they who were a threat to society and culture.

"If the world hates you, realize that it hated me first" (verse 18). All religious persecutions ultimately fail and produce a stronger Christianity than the one they tried to destroy. The Holy Spirit abides with the church and causes the courage so evident in the friends of Jesus. The world hates. Christians love. Church history shows that Christian love ultimately wins the battles.

Reflection

1. What do I know about vine planting customs in Christ's time?
2. What events at the Last Supper were good opportunities for Jesus to use the image of the vine and branches?
3. How does the vine-branch imagery help me develop intimacy with Jesus?
4. What are some stories I have that show how "branches" in my experience are headed for the "bonfire"?
5. I have worked on my relationships and keep the process going. What would be different in my relating to Jesus?
6. Why is obedience seldom spoken of today?
7. How would I describe Christian obedience?
8. Did Jesus choose me to be his friend because I was good and loveable? Explain. Relate this to divine grace.
9. Do I know of Christians who have suffered for standing up for their faith?
10. What causes "the world" to hate God and persecute Christians?

Prayer

Jesus Christ, vine of life and love, attach me as a fruitful branch to yourself, the life-source. Teach me the real meaning of Christian obedience and the context of love in which it is practiced. Send me your Holy Spirit to be my inner source of courage when I am called to stand up for my faith in you. Help me never to forget that without you I can do nothing that is in union with your redemptive purpose for the world.

16   Breathe on Us, Breath of God

The Divine Radiance of the Spirit's Light (Jn. 16:1-15)

A great shadow brooded over the Last Supper when Jesus outlined the sufferings the apostles would endure. His sobering words deflated them and caused them a mixture of fear and sadness. They felt dislocated when he predicted they would be expelled from the synagogues, those holy places where they absorbed the patriarchal faith, felt a spiritual bond with their families and friends, and acquired a sense of religious identity.

They shuddered at the harsh vision he painted for them when he told them they could anticipate being killed because of their commitment to his Gospel. And the ones who would kill them would believe they were virtually worshiping God in the process. At the very meal where their hearts had bounded with spiritual joy, the prospect of life-threatening situations depressed them with fear. Not only would they suffer, but do it alone without Jesus. The Master recognized their gloom. "Grief has filled your hearts" (verse 6).

But Christianity is not a religion for pessimists. Fashionable despair has never been the trademark of Christ's followers. Pain there will be, and death, but the process leads to hope and resurrection. That is why Jesus immediately followed his prediction of their troubles with his teaching about the coming of the Holy Spirit, God of light who would fill their being with radiance bright.

They would not face their challenges alone. The Spirit would come to them and Jesus would be near them through the Spirit. The great theme of light, so prevalent in John, would now apply to the action of the Spirit. Light was another way of talking about the divine glory, the act of God seeking ways to be intimately present to people. They would experience the Spirit as Truth, just as they had already encountered Jesus as Truth. From Jesus they had heard truths and experienced him as truly faithful to them. He witnessed the connection between truth and fidelity.

It is one thing to hear a truth, even accept it, and another matter to understand it. Thomas and Philip had listened to Jesus tell them the truth about the Way and the presence of the Father, but they barely knew what it meant. One day soon, the Spirit would come to them and open their minds to the rich meaning of these truths.

Knowing the meaning of Christ's truths would not be enough. Many bright Christians are skillful masters of the teachings of Jesus. They can recite them and deliver long and learned explanations of what they mean. But their approach is purely intellectual. They have knowledge without love. The truth in their minds has not gripped their hearts, emotions, and wills. It floats freely above their behavior and does not affect their lifestyle.

The mission of the Holy Spirit is twofold, to help us grasp the meaning of the truths of Jesus and show us how to translate those truths into love, fidelity, and Christian behavior. The Spirit is a masterful "uniter," a unifier. If we have an interior life that is compartmentalized — head here, heart there, will somewhere else, emotions disconnected — then we require a healing process to put it all together. We need an interior unification movement. That is what the Spirit wants to do for us.

Of course the Spirit can do nothing for us if we are not willing to accept the strong yet gentle unifying movement of love. This Spirit is light, glory, life, love, unity for us if we open ourselves to his influence. All those terms are different ways of describing the job the Spirit has been sent to do. They are all connected to that deceptively simply term Jesus used to console his nervous apostles, the term being "truth." "He will guide you to all truth" (verse 13).

Notice how resolutely supernatural and divine was the solution Jesus presented to his apostles. He did not try to minimize their fears. He accepted the fact that they were scared and confused. He did not provide them with reasonable escape routes from the terror ahead. He refused to have them pretend everything would be all right. He rejected offering them mental tricks to tide them through the rough seas. All the rationalizations the rest of us would think up, he repudiated.

Instead he lifted them to the highest levels of faith. Salvation is an act that originates from God and always is divine in its action. As an agent of this salvation, the Spirit of God would roam the whole earth and linger at the door of every human heart, ready to teach the meaning of Christ's truths and wrap into a marvelous unity the whole human person. Truth would become Love. Once that transformation took place, then the courage the apostles needed would immediately flow from their souls. Within an hour the apostles would run scared. But after Pentecost, armed with the Spirit, they would show how morally brave a person can be when God is in charge.

The Spirit and the Moral Law

The Spirit will also be the world's greatest consciousness raiser, a conscience trainer. The world will always try to forget the moral law. The frantic energies of the world will be used to block out the voice of conscience. But like a sonorous lawyer in the real courtroom of the planet, the human conscience, the Spirit will arouse moral awareness despite every secular effort to suppress it. This is why Jesus used the expression from the law courts, "convict!" The Spirit will "convict the world in regard to sin and righteousness and condemnation" (verse 8).

The word for convict here also means convince. Hence the Spirit works in two stages, first convincing, then convicting. Through convincing the Spirit brings our consciences to moral awareness and honesty. Through convicting, the Spirit judges the truth of the matter, and helps us come to the same conclusion. Because of the aggressive work of the Spirit pushing against every human conscience, the world's three great denials will be exposed.

The Denial of Evil

Terrible things happen everyday, yet the modern myth survives that evil does not exist. Nobody sins. Yes, maybe the evil occurs, but nobody is responsible. Social pressures from without and dark emotional drives from within wither away all moral responsibility — or so the culture claims. But the woman who spent a year at Auschwitz and saw her baby torn from her breast and fed to the gas ovens, ask her if evil exists. At the beginning of World War II, Albert Camus wrote, "The reign of the beasts has begun." He had the honesty to recognize evil when he saw it.

The massive denial of evil, despite all evidence to the contrary, is an insult to the intelligence of the human person, let alone a proud and implicit rejection of God. It tells people they are not responsible for their acts in any ultimate moral sense. Maybe what they did was a crime, a sin against the social order. Or perhaps it was due to madness, in which case it is no sin at all. But a conscious sin against God's moral laws? No way.

Jesus powerfully rejected this denial of sin. Why else was he here? The whole purpose of his incarnation, ministry, death on the cross, and resurrection from the dead was to save us from the sin that was all too evident to him. It is sin that is at the root of every other evil in the world. Genesis spelled that out in painful detail. Once the first parents sinned, the troubles in creation started. Revelation says that all the evils of the world are traceable to conscious and deliberate sin. To deny this is to reject a real assessment of the human condition — and to reject any need for salvation. Such a denial means that Christ's whole mission was useless.

The fact that there are always people who will rise up prophetically to make the world aware of its sinfulness, both social and individual, is evidence that the Spirit is at work. It is the Spirit who overcomes the denial of sin by awakening human conscience to this most deep seated of moral problems. We noted that the word that Jesus used for "convict" also means "convince." First the Spirit must convince human conscience of the truth of the reality of sin.

Then convict those who indeed have sinned and failed to repent. Who shall say there are not sins that cry to heaven for vengeance? Oppression of the poor, the single parents, widows, and street kids. Those who enslave others with drugs and alcohol. Those who cheat workers of their wages, old people of their pensions. Abusive parents and spouses. Is there not a sin against the Holy Spirit — the denial of sin through presumption, the surrender to sin which is despair?

Denial of the Need For Christ's Salvation

If there is no sin, there is no need of a savior. Why look for a redeemer when I have nothing to be redeemed from? This, despite the awesome record of evil. The first recorded death in the Bible resulted from a murder. Cain killed Abel. The creation of Genesis has become *de-creation* in the twentieth century as the so-called advanced nations (the ones usually denying the need for a savior) extinguished millions of their own sons and daughters in World War I. In addition, the modern world has attempted four major genocides: the Jews in the holocaust, the Ukrainians in the forced famine, the Armenians by a bloodbath, and the Cambodians by systematic murder. And when the West spawned a "savior," it was the anti-savior, James Jones, who led his people to mass suicide on a tropical settlement at Jonestown.

Jesus had never committed a crime. He never committed a sin. He taught love and inspired hope. He healed people and consoled them in their sorrows. He was likeable and loveable. He stood for all that was decent and humane. Children loved him. He was the most likely candidate to be a savior. But because deep within humanity there is a tendency to deny the need for a savior (just as there is an equal hunger to have a savior). that dark side of the human spirit prevailed.

When such a denial overcomes the fundamental desire for salvation, then the forces of evil gather and destroy the object of their hatred. Denial is an unhealthy attitude. When it takes the form of hostile aggression, it becomes deadly. Denial for the need of a savior released a rush of evil impulses which rapidly joined forces to kill Jesus. A coalition of Jewish and Roman leaders connected and brought about the crucifixion of Jesus. The best person in the world was visibly killed as a criminal. The greatest upholder of justice was executed as one who had performed an injustice.

Denial of the need for Jesus as savior has had equally fatal consequences in contemporary times. Just as the Romans did all they could to liquidate Christians — and therefore, Christ — so the modern states have used the awesome power provided by technology's weapons to hunt, kill and oppress Christians in Central and Eastern Europe, China and Vietnam. More subtly, the free cultures of the West practice the same denial by picking away at Christian belief in a thousand ways. Blood martyrdom on the one hand and dry martyrdom on the other.

That is just it! The Spirit has raised up witnesses to faith in the need for salvation above all where the opposition is greatest. Militant atheism-triumphant has proved to be the sham it always was, and now its most ardent advocates are abandoning the idea. The divine "attorney" has breathed the spirit of faith into millions of people, kept alive the consciences of believers in gulags, death camps, jungle prisons, in the homes of the poor, and the citadels of the mighty. If the human conscience is a field, the Spirit is its most favorite farmer. If conscience is the world's permanent courtroom, the Spirit is its most active lawyer, exposing radical denials and calling people to honesty and truth. Jesus is indeed our Redeemer.

The Denial of Satan

The Holy Spirit as lawyer has one more conviction to make, that of Satan. Jesus foretold that by the Spirit "the ruler of this world has been condemned" (verse 11). But before the conviction, there must be the convincing. The Spirit must awaken human conscience to the reality of Satan and overcome the pervasive denial of his presence. C.S. Lewis has written the best book on this subject of denial of Satan. His *Screwtape Letters*, is a brilliant and humorous, yet deadly serious, explosion of the modern myth that there is no devil. The world tries to convince believers that Satan is a myth. A comic character drawn from the mists of legend, fantasy and pre-industrial superstition. This denial of Satan is in reality the comforting myth of the upscale modern, too sophisticated to believe in such nonsense, too educated to be bothered with silly stories about the devil.

As Lewis points out, that is just the way Satan wants it. The Father of Lies is happiest when his "big lie" works. The theory of the big lie is that the more you tell it, the more people will believe it. Biblical people had no trouble believing in Satan, though they never made him an equal of God as some other ancient religions did. The Bible calls him a lion, a wolf, a dragon and a serpent, but above all, a fallen angel. Jesus refers to him as the "Ruler of this World," the "Prince of Darkness." In the epistles he is the chief one among the evil "principalities and powers." The evidence is so extensive that it is a wonder that some believers could be persuaded that Satan is not present today.

The eighteenth century Age of Reason, or Enlightenment, had much to do with creating the modern myth of the denial of Satan. But the horrors of the twentieth century and the dissolution of the optimistic "myth of progress through science and technology" has created the environment in which the Holy Spirit can convince contemporary conscience of the presence of this dangerous source of evil. In Christ's time Satan's purpose was to destroy Jesus. The Lord spoke of this, "The ruler of the world is coming. He has no power over me" (Jn. 14:30). Satan has the same purpose today.

The Spirit is at work in our consciences arousing them to an awareness of the fatal temptations of Satan. The "ruler of the world" wants to rule our souls, dividing us from Christ, from one another and from all those we love. The word devil means divider. Once the Spirit can convince us, he can convict Satan. We must permit the

Spirit to make our consciences sensitive to this dangerous presence. Exposed, Satan can be convicted. Denied, he makes us his victims. The first choice is better.

A Lesson From a Woman in Labor (Jn. 16:16-33)

To help them cope with the troubles ahead, Jesus gave them a divine teaching about the Spirit's powerful presence and action. He followed that up with a familiar human image. A woman in labor suffers pain and anxiety, but she suffers in hope. "When a woman is in labor, she is in anguish because her hour has arrived; but when she has given birth to a child, she no longer remembers the pain because of her joy that a child has been born into the world (verse 21). The screams and tears of a woman in labor will be followed by her laughter and clear-eyed joy.

The theme of pain and struggle as the prelude to joy and the source of hope is as common in secular wisdom as it is in Christ's teachings. T-shirts sport the axioms: No pain — No gain. No guts. No glory. The Latin proverb echoes the same truth. "Per aspera ad astra." (Through the struggles — To the stars). Those are the little sayings of perennial common sense.

Most people wish the process were otherwise. They prefer a painless path to glory and happiness. They declare, defensively and aggressively, that life should be easy. They read dozens of self-help books that assure them the road to salvation is simple and easy. They listen to the Dr. Feelgood's and Dr. Goodvibes — modern versions of snake-oil salesmen — who confidently peddle yet another quick fix for the restless people who refuse to face the pain and discipline needed to mature psychologically and spiritually.

Jesus was clearly not against people feeling happy. "I will see you again and your hearts will rejoice and no one will take your joy away from you" (verse 22). But he delivered the tough message that hope and joy are found in taking the path of suffering that alone leads to the desired happiness. His message would sound stern and cold if he did not balance it with the assurance of hope, peace, joy, and fulfillment. His words would leave us desolate if he did not show how it worked in his own life and promise us the Spirit's presence so we did not walk alone. The divine comedy has a tragic phase. Exactly. A phase, not a dead end. "Those that sow in tears shall reap rejoicing" (Ps. 126:5).

Reflection

1. How can the Spirit unite my inner life?
2. Jesus said the Spirit would guide me into all truth. What are the two aspects of truth I will experience from the Spirit?
3. How does the Spirit affect my conscience as "convincer" and "convicter"?
4. What are some examples of the denial of evil and sin which I note from my experience?
5. How can I tell that some people deny the need for a savior?
6. In my faith development what has been my reaction to the existence and presence of Satan?
7. How does the Spirit "convince" and "convict" human awareness of sin, salvation, and Satan?
8. What are some everyday bits of wisdom I learned from my parents, relatives, and friends about the connection between pain, discipline, struggle and the search for hope and happiness and fulfillment?
9. What two assurances do we have from Jesus about the essential link between sorrow and joy?
10. What quick fixes have I used to avoid the difficult road to hope and joy?

Prayer

Holy Spirit, divine "attorney," you can help me overcome the denials of sin, the need for a savior and the presence of Satan. Convince my conscience of the true realities. Lead me to the conviction that is a judgement on sin, a judgement on the "ruler" of this world, and the faith I need to believe in Jesus along with the community of believers, the church.

17   Jesus Prays for Us

A Little Bit of Heaven (Jn. 17:1-8)

At the Last Supper Jesus spoke of his Father forty-five times. He had drawn his apostles to realize that the Father was as close and available to them as the Son who sat and ate with them. "Whoever has seen me has seen the Father" (Jn. 14:9). Jesus helped them to see that God was more than an impersonal force "up there." God was a Father who is "right here." People through all of history have tended to keep God at a distance, pushing him to a world beyond the skies. Then, with no apologies for the contradictory attitude, people demand that God be as near as a beloved friend.

Too many people box up God as an idea, an impersonal force, ominously powerful, too far away to be caring, too busy with the galaxies to worry about the everyday troubles of mothers with sick children, a husband fearful of losing his job, a teacher despairing of his students, a grandmother battling melanoma, a homeowner scraping up mortgage payments.

Those who promote the abstract God may like this approach because this keeps the divine under control. They smooth the wrinkles out of God's face and make him bland enough to be harmless — and irrelevant. Drained of blood, the body of this God is a distant "something" that has no impact on people.

Jesus spoke for those who hunger for a God who cares for people. Jesus used family language when talking of God. God is a lot more than a force. God is a Father. There are family ties between God the Son and God the Father. Better yet, there is a familial connection between the Father and all his daughters and sons on earth. The "My Father" of Jesus is the "Our Father" of the human race.

Around the family table of the final Passover, Jesus made visible the presence of the greatest patriarch of all, the affectionate Father of each human being. Jesus became positively lyrical at this moment wnen revealing the presence of his Father at the "head of the table" of the banquet of life.

The only explicit reference in the gospels to Jesus singing is at the Last Supper (see Mk. 14:26). The text of John 17 has such a melodic quality that it is quite possible it was used as a Eucharistic hymn by the early Christians, almost like the Preface of the Catholic Mass today. If then Jesus ever were to be heard singing, it was because he was so delighted to reveal his Father to the family.

In the ecstasy of those last intimate moments with his closest friends on earth, Jesus sang, "I revealed your name to those whom you gave me out of the world" (verse 8). Philosophers use reason to speak of an impersonal God. Jesus used revelation to tell us that God s as personal as a caring Father. "I revealed your name."

Jesus brought the glory of the Father to the simplicity of the Last Supper table. In the synoptic gospels Jesus often compared heaven to a joyous dinner party. In John's gospel, Jesus transformed the Passover Meal into a foretaste of heaven. Precisely through the eventful, last splendid meal, Jesus could gesture to the table and then to the community around it and say, "Now this is eternal life, that they should know you, the only true God, and the one whom you have sent, Jesus Christ" (verse 3). Through the simple reality of a celebratory feast, Jesus offered them — and us — a revelation of heaven.

This is the mood, the scene, the holy environment in which we should hear his words about heaven. This is the context of understanding his description of heaven as "knowing" our Father. The verb "to know" in Hebrew means love knowledge, not simply book knowledge. In heaven we do not know about the Father, like a biologist looking at a specimen. We know our Father. In heaven we would do more than stand at a reverential distance and shyly peek at the glory. No. There we are grasped by our Father with the kind of love we have always dreamed of. This is a knowledge replenished with everlasting affection. Now that is "eternal" life.

Jesus tells us there is more to be said. Eternal life begins here. Heaven starts on earth. At the Last Supper Jesus did not speak in the future tense, but the present one. He did not say that one day they would know the Father and then enter eternal life. Nothing so vague and promissory for Jesus. Right then in that room, the experience has already begun.

Jesus has introduced them that evening to his Father and theirs. The glory fills that little room. This is the start of a heavenly journey that will have its consummation permanently in life after death. In just a few days Jesus would enter into that glory forever. In just a few years, so would they. And that is the same for us.

Time stood still on that Holy Night which began with the washing of the feet and the communion with Jesus through the living bread and the great cup. Why? Because the experience of eternity replaced it.

Jesus Prays for the Apostles (Jn. 17:9-19)

Jesus proceeded to pray for his apostles. Addressing his Father he offered three petitions for them: Keep them in love. Keep them from evil. Consecrate them in truth. Each petition deserves a brief reflection here.

Keep Them in Love. Normally, we think of praying to Jesus, or to the Father through Jesus. The emphasis here is on Jesus praying to the Father for the apostles, and us by extension. His first petition concerns the unity in love which the apostles must preserve. He had commanded them to love as he did, meaning they should love in such a way that they brought God into the lives of others. Their love should always have a salvation purpose. Apostolic love must always have a spiritual goal. This is no sentimental love such as romantic dreamers espouse. It is a demanding love. Often there will be little pleasure to it, rather mortal danger. James will be beheaded. Peter will be jailed and crucified. All of them will be expelled from the synagogue communities which had meant so much to them.

They will have to become a new community, the Christian church. As the pillars of this new church, they must witness unity and love. Jesus prayed to the Father "that they may be one just as we are" (verse 11). Each apostle is meant to be a sign of the unity of the church. Taken together the community of apostles themselves should constitute a collective witness of the unity which is expected of the whole of God's people. The words of Jesus about unity have been applied today to the ecumenical movement — an excellent application — but they were first spoken to the Father about the apostles. Jesus expected unity from them and prayed, as he still does, for the unity of the apostles and their successors, the pope and bishops.

Keep Them From Evil. In the Our Father, Jesus taught us to say, "deliver us from evil." In many ways, Christ's prayer for his apostles sounds like the Our Father, especially this petition, "Keep them from the evil one" (verse 15). What kind of evil? Certainly not persecution. He did not choose "soft men" to be apostles. He picked a hardy lot and toughened them up spiritually during the years he trained them. When describing the eight attitudes for spiritual happiness he ended up with a daunting challenge. "Blessed are you when they insult you and persecute you and utter every kind of evil against you because of me" (Mt. 5:11).

Jesus did not pray that they be delivered from the indignities of persecution and martyrdom. He prayed that they be protected from the evil of sin. They could never be messengers of salvation if they led a life of sin. Then they would be the morally blind leading the morally blind. If they did not exhibit in their personal lives the moral integrity that resulted from the saving grace of Jesus, then their message would be hypocritical in the extreme.

A scandalous apostle would demoralize the church and cause people to fall away from faith. Sad to say, many shepherds of the church during the course of its history have indeed surrendered to sin and caused infidelity among the faithful. Jesus was not praying for saints, but for pilgrims, weak apostles who would need divine assistance to carry out the demanding mission to which they were called.

Consecrate Them in Truth. Jesus had trained the apostles to be missionaries of the Gospel. He planned to send them the Holy Spirit who would transform the meager clay of their present weakness into the full bodied life of evangelical power. The Holy Spirit would lead them to holiness. The experience would be like the Old Testament's anointing of prophets, priests and kings. The physical oil of anointing was an image of the invisible transformation caused by the Spirit. Here, Jesus as high priest was talking to his apostles as the anointed men called to identify with the holy.

When Jesus spoke here of "consecration" he was referring to holiness, a term that refers to the inner beauty of God. What quality above all has attracted men and women of every age to seek God? The divine beauty. What finally convinces the human heart that communion with God is the greatest of all goals? The beauty of God. Divine holiness has two sides to it: (1). The moral purity that induces a virtuous life in those who want to be identified with God. (2). The inherent attractiveness of beauty that needs no arguments to draw the heart to surrender and communion.

A snow-capped mountain peak does not need to plead its case, "Come to me and love me." The movement of the stars has never caused anyone to debate such magnificence. The boundless sweep of the ocean requires no arguments to draw attention. Nature's wonders speak for themselves and attract without force. Neither does the beauty of God once it is perceived. St. Augustine wrote that tourists will travel the ends of the earth to behold nature's magnificence, "Yet they leave themselves unnoticed. They do not marvel at themselves" (*Confessions* 10, 8).

He went on to say that we cannot hope to find God until we find ourselves. The human tragedy is to be driven outward, to lose touch with ourselves and wander far from our hearts. Such was Augustine's own life journey until he found God who drew him into divine intimacy with a passion. For him the drawing power of God was his beauty. "Too late have I loved you, O Beauty ever ancient and ever new! Too late I loved you! And, behold, you were within me, and I out of myself, and there I searched for you" (*Confessions* 9,12). That beauty is another name for God's holiness. It charmed Augustine enough that for forty years of his life as a priest and bishop, he journeyed as deeply as any saint ever did into the warm embrace of God's holiness.

Such is the experience Jesus had in mind when he prayed that the apostles be consecrated in truth. He had awakened them to a sense of their inner lives and revealed to them his own inexpressible beauty, his glory. They clearly had trouble understanding his teachings, but they were in no doubt that they wanted to be near him and follow him as his disciples. The process of consecration had already begun. Jesus prayed to the Father that it continue and that the Spirit would bring it to maturity.

Jesus connected holiness with truth. True holiness cannot be based on a myth or on an illusion. Jesus did not spend his years spinning useless fantasies for his listeners. He taught the truth because he knew that truth was the best nourishment for the soul. What he said about God was true. Moreover, Jesus claimed to be the living truth, meaning his evident fidelity to each human being. He was true to people. Thus he embodied truth in his person. Holiness is identity with God who is both true and faithful.

Then Jesus Prayed for Us (Jn. 17: 20-28)

Having prayed so fervently for his first missionaries, Jesus then gazed into the future and prayed for the people who will be evangelized. The apostles will call them to belief in him — as messiah and Son of God. The outstanding gift he prayed for was unity. "That they may all be one, as you, Father, are in me and I in you" (verse 21). Why should they have this unity? "That the world may believe that you sent me" (verse 21).

This unity would have two aspects.

(1). Christians should be united to God with an intimacy like that of the Son and the Father.

(2). Secondly, Christians should be united to one another with love, care, mercy, justice, and kindness.

Both types of unity are essential. To be united to God with no interest in mutual love for one another would be a travesty. It would be nothing more than supernatural narcissism. It would fail to be true Christianity, because there would be no charitable witness. It would cease to be real spirituality because it would prove to be illusory. A concentration on God without affection for people eventually becomes a morbid preoccupation with a self imagining it is in touch with God.

On the other hand, the quest for a fellowship group with no reference to God is equally doomed. Such people wind up in a fruitless quest for just the right, friendly group. Forever, they either expel the so-called colorless or abrasive members or else they run off to another group that seems a bit more charming and bright minded. These people are looking for clubs not a church.

Jesus intended only one Christian Church. The unity would be modeled on the unity of Father, Son and Spirit and would reflect the love that binds the persons of the Trinity. The unity within the church would be made possible by the power of the Spirit, therefore, being caused by a divine power. Christians have split apart in the course of history. Today it is clearer that Christians have a moral obligation to seek the unity for which Christ prayed at the Last Supper. The ecumenical movement is the result of a grace given to Christians of these times.

Vatican II's Decree on Ecumenism has responded to Christ's call to unity among Christians. "The restoration of unity among all Christians is one of the principal concerns of the Second Vatican Council. Christ the Lord founded one church and one church only. However, many Christian communions present themselves as true inheritors of Jesus Christ. All indeed profess to be followers of the Lord but they differ in mind and go their different ways as if Christ himself were divided. Certainly such division openly contradicts the will of Christ, scandalizes the world, and damages that most holy cause, the preaching of the Gospel to every creature."*

But there is not only division among the churches, there is also disunity within the churches, including Catholicism. The ascendancy of a political vision of faith has caused people to be divided along lines more common to secular states than a Christian community. The politicizing of theology, church discipline and pastoral practice threatens to scatter the people of God into new splinter groups. Playing politics with Jesus and the Christian community is a new scandal that needs to be confronted as vigorously as the old division among churches.

The relevance of Christ's prayer for unity at the Last Supper has never been more acute. Quarrels within the church weaken its witness, distract it from its evangelical mission and dilute its energies. Such disputes divert the attention of pastors and parishioners from the priorities of lives that should be focused on Jesus the Savior and loving compassion for one another. Unless there is a return to a resolutely spiritual focus, the politicizing of Christians will enervate what is left of faith and eliminate what survives of love. Jesus prayed that we would be united to God and to one another in the loving power of the Spirit. In such a way did Jesus conclude his farewell address to his apostles. The majesty of the Great Sermon and Prayer of the Last Supper has never seemed more resplendent or relevant to Christian lives. We owe much to the artistry of St. John who remembered and saved these words of Jesus for our instruction and inspiration.

At the end we are drawn to silence. We gaze on that little group around the Master as they lift the final cup of wine for the last toast of Passover. The room seems too small for the greatness it contains.

---

*"Decree on Ecumenism," *Unitatis Redintegratio, Vatican Council II: Conciliar and Post Conciliar Documents*, Austin Flannery, ed. (Northport, NY: Costello Publishing Co., 1981).

The air too soft for the ringing truths that Jesus uttered. The night too dark for the light that shines from the visible Son and the invisible Father at that table. But that is God's way, to embody the greatest reality in the simplest of settings.

The drama of the passion is about to begin.

"Get up. Let us go" (Jn. 14:31).

Reflection

1. Many people think of God as far away in heaven. How could I help them see God is right here?
2. Why do people want to keep God abstract instead of being a personal, caring Father?
3. Why did Jesus like to use festive meals as images of what heaven is like? How does eternal life begin here?
4. Jesus prayed that the Father keep the apostles in his love. What kind of love does Jesus mean?
5. Why is it important that the Father keep the apostles from evil?
6. What does holiness suggest to me? Why is holiness as beauty a good way to speak of God's holiness?
7. People travel everywhere to behold the world's marvels. Why do they so seldom marvel at the inner wonders of their souls?
8. Jesus prayed for the unity of Christians. What happens when Christians only work on being united to God, but not each other?
9. What happens when Christians spend their energies building fellowship with each other, but pay no attention to union with God?
10. How do I advance the cause of ecumenism? How do I approach the disunity within the church caused by politicizing?

Prayer

Jesus you made it clear that your Father is a personal and caring God and that eternal life is knowing the Father in a loving manner. You gave us the example of how to pray and what to pray for. You have asked the Father to grant us the gift of unity — a unity with God and among ourselves. And all this in the setting of the Eucharist. I praise you for these gifts which I will share with others.

18 The Passover Moon Over the Halls of Injustice

Passover moon now shed your silver glow
Upon the City — its Savior soon to know.

The Arrest and the First Trial (Jn. 18:1-25)

Jesus and his disciples left the Upper Room, walked down
Mount Zion — on which Jerusalem stood — and crossed the Kidron
brook. They climbed up the Mount of Olives to the Garden of
Gethsemane. The mountainside was filled with enclosed gardens
owned by families in Jerusalem. This quiet retreat belonged to a
friend of Christ's, and he often went there for meetings with his
disciples (verse 2). Judas guessed that Jesus would be there and came
with soldiers and guards carrying torches and weapons.

John's gospel does not have the account of the Agony of Jesus in
the Garden, but he does report that a "troubled" Jesus surrendered to
the Father's will in 12:27-32.

Jesus went out to meet Judas and the arrest party. He was not
laid back or fearful. He was a commanding presence bent on
defeating the forces of evil and sin in the world. His passion was not
a passive capitulation to social forces, but rather an act of will, a
show of moral and spiritual strength. He did not just let things
happen to him. As a person of character he made events serve his
purposes. He was the "Lord of battles," as the psalms would put it.
At the very outset of the passion, John emphasizes this truth about
Jesus. He is always the Lord.

Hence we see that it was Jesus who confronted the troops, not
the arrest party crashing in on him. He went out to meet them and
asked them, "Whom are you looking for?" They replied, "Jesus the
Nazarean." He said to them, "I AM" (see verses 4-5).

Ever since God had revealed his name as I AM to Moses at the burning bush, there was always an experience of awe in the listeners. Constantly, throughout John's gospel, Jesus applied this name to himself, identifying himself with God. The traitor and the troops had come to arrest Jesus. They found themselves encountering a mysterious force — the Lord. All of them fell back in awe before the Lord.

But Jesus had no intention of paralyzing them with the eternal might of God. He gave them an experience of awe, not to show off divine muscle, but as always to invite them to faith in his total person. Awe can be and should be the beginning of faith wisdom. He gave them a chance to freely accept the real Jesus. They failed.

He told them not to touch his disciples. The shepherd protected his flock. But Peter took a sword and cut off the right ear of Malchus, a servant of the high priest. Jesus moved swiftly to stop this violence. He immediately healed Malchus (Lk. 22:51) and ordered Peter to put away the sword. "Shall I not drink the cup that the Father has given me?" (verse 11). Peter chose violence — the sword. Jesus sided with non-violence — the cup of vulnerability.

Remember that Christ's vulnerability was not that of a soft man, a wimp letting people push him around. His was the vulnerability of a man of ethical character allowing suffering to happen to him in pursuit of a higher goal, the triumph of love and forgiveness over hatred and evil. Pain was not an end in itself. That would be masochism. It was a means to a goal. That is salvation. Jesus used soul power against the world's swords and clubs to achieve his purposes. He was showing all of them how to change the love of power into the power of love.

The soldiers took Jesus to the house of Annas. Accompanied by "the other disciple," Peter followed the marching men. The text says this "other disciple" was an acquaintance of Annas and used his contact and influence to gain entrance for him and Peter into the courtyard of the house where the two of them could await the outcome of the trial. This "other disciple" was John the apostle.

The spring night was cold. Peter and John joined the servants and guards around the fire to keep warm. A maid asked Peter if he were a follower of Jesus. Peter denied it. The courageous warrior of Gethsemane had suddenly collapsed. Even John's presence could not sustain his moral strength. He did not yet have the inner ethical discipline to stand up for Jesus.

Inside the house Annas questioned Jesus about his doctrine.
Jesus told them that his teachings were public and well known. He
had no secret teachings. He spoke openly in the synagogues and
temple. Let them ask his listeners what he said. At this a temple
guard slapped Jesus and accused him of being insolent. Jesus asked
the guard why he hit him. If he had spoken the truth honestly there
was no reason to strike him. But the truth often offends and hurts
those who hear it. They retaliate by hurting the one who speaks it.
Annas closed the hearing by having Jesus tied up and sent to Caiphas.

Peter stayed close to the fire to keep warm. Someone else asked
him if he were a disciple of Jesus. He said, "I am not." Finally, a
relative of Malchus, the man whose ear he had cut off, said that he
saw Peter in the garden with Jesus. Peter denied his Lord for the
third time. And the cock crowed. Thus Peter proved that Jesus knew
him better than he knew himself. He had thought of himself as a
brave man. In a sense he was, if it meant physical battle. But when it
came to the deeper struggle, the inner moral war he was expected to
fight, he failed. He did not yet have the interior moral discipline to
win such encounters with himself.

To be strong on the outside is not a guarantee one will be strong
on the inside. Ultimately, a person with true inner power, will be
strong outwardly, not only in a physical way, but also in a moral and
spiritual manner. Soul power on the inside will become soul power
on the outside. Peter's tears will bring about the start of his inner
conversion. That conversion will be completed when he is saved by
the cross of Jesus and the coming of the Holy Spirit into his soul.

The Trial Before Pilate Begins (Jn. 18:28-40)

On Good Friday morning they brought Jesus to Pilate's house,
the Fortress Antonia, also called the Praetorium. Pilate normally
lived in a palace at Jericho, but at Passover he used his town house in
Jerusalem to keep an eye on the crowds so he could quickly
supervise and control any political troubles or rebellions. The street
in front of his house was a typically narrow thoroughfare to be found
in ancient cities, with the exception of an assembly area, the size of a
tennis court, just in front of his residence. It was called the
lithostrotos or stone pavement.

Today the Sisters of Zion have a convent at this site and their building covers the lithostrotos. Christian art has influenced movie representations of this scene causing us to imagine it as an area the size of a football field where thousands of demonstrators gathered in front of a marble columned stage. The reality was much simpler and downscaled to a relatively small situation. Pilate's house was far closer to 10 Downing Street than to Buckingham Palace. Or in American terms, to Blair House as contrasted with the White House.

Moreover, the crowd was probably not more than a few hundred people at most. Not only was there not room for a cast of thousands, but it was also just dawn and the speed of events precluded the organizing of any kind of huge turnout. Of course the size of the crowd and the expanse of the assembly area is not the real point of the account. A gathering of a few hundred people was just as capable of influencing the tragic outcome as would a mob of one hundred thousand. Pilate wanted no public disturbances big or small. In that volatile period a spark was as dangerous as a torch.

In John's narrative, the trial before Pilate occurs in seven scenes, four of them outside the Antonia and four inside the residence. The rhythm of the scene changes matching the mounting tension and the inexorable progress toward the final condemnation of Jesus. The Jews on the outside and the Romans on the inside finally collude in the death sentence for Jesus. But we should remember they are but surrogates for us. It was the sins of the whole human race that motivated Jesus to undergo the brutality of the Passion. We all share in the responsibility for the passion, not by being physically present there, but because of our sinfulness that participates in the evil that caused Christ's Passion in the first place.

At the same time the search for blame is an unfitting attitude in our contemplation of the passion. Jesus himself set the tone with his first word from the cross. "Father, forgive them, they know not what they do" (Lk. 24:34). We come not to judge those involved in the process of the passion, but to tell the story and see how it speaks to our own hearts of the need for personal conversion.

Scene One: Execute Jesus! (Outside). The Jews came to the Antonia but would not enter Pilate's residence because that would cause them ceremonial defilement to go inside the house of a gentile. They would not be able to eat at the Passover table in such a state. So Pilate came out to meet them. He was the sixth Roman governor of Judea since the conquest and was now in his tenth year of office.

Jews hated him automatically because he was the head of the Roman occupation.

They also despised him because he had sacrilegiously defiled their temple by hanging a portrait of the emperor there. Their religion forbade the making of pictures of people or carved statues of people or animals similar to pagan idols (graven images). The most serious of sins would be to try to make an image of God, hence to put a picture of a pagan in their most holy place was an exceedingly inflammatory act.

So reverent were they about even saying the name of God — let alone picturing him — that they used synonyms instead. Only the high priest could publicly utter God's name once a year at the Feast of Atonement.

Adding insult to injury, Pilate also raided the temple treasury — took God's funds — to finance the building of an aqueduct to serve the city. Let him take taxes (they grudgingly paid), but let him not touch the funds for God's house. His ruthless and insensitive act caused a series of unstoppable violent demonstrations where the people bared their necks and welcomed the sword rather than have such an abomination in their temple. During this uprising some Galileans were killed. Rome concluded that Pilate had created too great a problem over a religious issue where the government tended to be tolerant of provincial wishes, so he was ordered to back down.

Unpalatable as it may have been to deal with Pilate, the religious leaders and their followers had no other choice if they wanted to eliminate Jesus. He possessed the "jus gladii" (the right of the sword) meaning that only he could order an execution. Their hostility to Jesus overcame their negative feelings about Pilate.

Why were they so against Jesus? The priests were profoundly offended by what they considered his blasphemous identification with divinity — even to the point of presuming to forgive sins. The Pharisees intensely disliked his criticism of their religious externalism and his defiance of sabbath laws to heal people. The scribes were wounded by his exposure of their simple minded literalism in explaining the Scriptures. The sophisticated Sadducees were still fuming about his authoritative defense of the resurrection of the body, a teaching they denied.

The priests should have been more intent on making God's presence felt among the people. When the glory-presence of the

Word made flesh came among them, he was an indictment of their own failure. The Pharisees should have advocated a covenant lifestyle similar to that of the prophets whose heirs they were. Jesus, the ultimate prophet, was a reproach to them. The scribes should have interpreted the Scriptures with the wisdom of the sages, freeing Scripture to speak of God's life among their people. Christ's exuberant opening of the vitality of the Word of God exposed the pitiable explanations they were presenting.

The Sadducees should have sensed God's care for the whole human person, body as well as spirit, hence God's promise of the body's resurrection. Their upscale lifestyle (pampering the body) blinded them to the body's real future potential. Jesus was unsparing with them. When he raised Lazarus from the dead, he offered them the first witness of the greater reality of a permanent resurrection. To make sure no one could miss the point, he said, "I AM the resurrection and the life" (Jn. 11:25).

So Pilate obtained his first glimpse of Jesus surrounded by the religious establishment whom he had alienated in a variety of ways. Not only had he been a living reproach to their shortcomings, he threatened to upset the social order over which they enjoyed control. In their eyes he was a political threat as well as a religious one. They saw him as a loose cannon who must be killed.

Scene Two: Kingdom and Truth (Inside). Pilate went back into his house and summoned Jesus for a private conference. It was immediately clear to the governor that Jesus was not a typical prisoner. Jesus had a disarming presence, not obviously threatening. This was no wild-eyed rebel leader like Judas the Galilean who mounted the ill-fated tax revolt. This was the man who compelled his own chief lieutenant, Peter, to give up using swords. This was a man whose face was full of bruises and cuts from the beating at the house of Annas. This quiet dignified man cared nothing for armed force and talked of his kingdom in spiritual terms.

Normally Pilate wasted little time on court cases and he was never known to have actually become a defender of an accused person. But Jesus was different. He did not stand before Pilate passively — nor yet defiantly. He treated Pilate like every other human being, one capable of redemption, one worthy of his effort to convert him to faith.

Pilate knew he had to clear up this kingdom matter. "Are you the king of the Jews?" (verse 33). Jesus replied that his kingdom was spiritual, not a worldly political one. Trained in the uses of power and institutional thinking, Pilate continued to press Jesus on the king issue. So Christ's kingdom is spiritual. Does that mean he is king of such a realm? Jesus explained that he is a king of truth. His role as king was to witness to truth.

We should recall again here Christ's discussion of truth with his apostles at the Last Supper the night before. When he spoke of truth he included both the truth of his teachings as well as his personal fidelity to God, self and others as the way he lived and personalized the truth. Truth is attainable and can be taught and learned. Truth is arrived at both from revelation and from thinking with one's mind. Revealed truth and reasoned truth do not contradict each other. Truth is truth regardless of the source.

A spiritual kingdom is based on truth, which when it is witnessed and lived, is a form of love. Truth in the mind is an idea. Truth in the heart is love. A spiritual life is possible for us because it flows from truth. That is why the church has always stressed the importance of doctrine — the truth of Christ's teaching — as well as the importance of a philosophy which affirms that truth can be known. Relativism in modern culture claims that there is no truth, only opinions more or less credible. This affects church people when they are persuaded to ignore or downplay doctrinal teaching, Christ's truth, as unimportant or simply one opinion among many in the so-called marketplace of ideas. If the reality of truth can be undermined, then the reality of the spiritual life can be rejected. Deny the possibility of knowing truth and we will fail to enter the kingdom of Jesus, a spiritual kingdom.

As Jesus gazed on Pilate, he saw a man deeply trapped in pure pragmatism. He encountered a ruler whose philosophy was, "To be personal was to be political." Compromise, power plays, strategies, fearful watchfulness, ruthless action, pretense, vanity, show, survival, these elements of political life were his daily bread. He had politicized his thinking to the point where his brain was virtually dead when confronted with the possibility that there was such a reality as truth, and that some people actually lived by the truth they believed. He would become one of history's best remembered relativists. Jesus reached out to him and offered him the hope of change. But all that Pilate could do was to revert to form and speak his cynical question, starkly recorded in John's gospel.

"What is truth?" (verse 38).

Scene Three: Barabbas Chosen (Outside). The wily mind of this provincial governor was not open to Christ's appeal to truth. But Jesus did touch some mysterious part of Pilate's heart. For once in his life Pilate felt a touch of sympathy for someone brought to his court. Some dim feeling inside him told him the man was innocent, a kind of harmless dreamer. Actually it was Christ's talk about truth that hit a positive chord in Pilate, for every human being has been created to know truth, live by it and thrive in it.

Pilate decided to use the Privilegium Paschale, the custom of the Passover amnesty as a move to free Jesus. A well known revolutionary named Barabbas was presently in custody. Since both Jesus and Barabbas were being detained for the same alleged crime — though the accusation was clearly true in the case of Barabbas — Pilate judged that the two of them would be presented to the people. He hoped they would pick Jesus and let him go free. He even spoke up on behalf of Jesus. "I find no guilt in him" (verse 38).

But the people had been politicized by the religious leaders. Propaganda replaced truth. Emotion prevailed over reason. Hostility blocked compassion. "The chief priests and the elders persuaded the crowds to ask for Barabbas but to destroy Jesus" (Mt. 27:20). Pilate took a poll and was given the impressionistic outcome of this way of doing justice. Pilate relied on a vote to arrive at truth and justice. Poll taking and voting, given the circumstances, were poor substitutes for honesty and truth. At Passover a lamb was slain for sinful people. Barabbas the sinner went free. Jesus the innocent lamb went to his death.

Reflection

1. Jesus was not passive in his passion. He made events serve his saving purpose. How do I actively make my life serve my goals?
2. How do I allow myself to be vulnerable? In what way do I put this at the service of my spiritual goals?
3. Peter was physically brave on the outside. What was missing inside him that led him to deny Jesus?
4. Why is inner ethical discipline necessary for me in order that my outer behavior might be moral and spiritual?

5. In what broad sense do I share responsibility for the passion of Jesus?
6. Why were the priests, Pharisees, scribes and Sadducees so dedicated to eliminating Jesus?
7. Pilate had extreme difficulty in appreciating what Jesus meant by truth. What difficulties might I have with truth? Or people I know?
8. What is the link between truth and Christ's kingdom?
9. What was there about Jesus that changed Pilate's usual attitude toward prisoners brought before him?
10. Why was poll taking and voting a bad idea when trying to get justice for Jesus in the scene with Barabbas?

Prayer

Jesus, King of truth, your spiritual kingdom is based on a true reality. You offered Pilate the possibility of faith conversion founded on truth in terms of teachings and faithful behavior. Put your light in my mind that I may see the truth and your love in my heart that I might live the truth.

19   When I Survey the Wondrous Cross

The Trial Before Pilate, Continued (Jn. 19:1-16)

Scene Four: Christ is Scourged, Crowned, Mocked (Inside).
Pilate was reluctant to order the execution of Jesus. In his perverse way, he judged that submitting Jesus to a severe beating would gain the pity of the people. Once they beheld his battered body, they would relent and call the whole thing off. The Passover Amnesty had not worked. Pilate's own testimony about Christ's innocence was rejected. Now he would appeal to their tender mercies.

A scourging customarily preceded crucifixion. It was meant to weaken the victim so that he would die sooner on the cross. The scourge was a leather whip. At its tip was a piece of lead whose weight increased the impact of the lash. Sometimes the ankle bone of a sheep was added to the tip of the lash. Its jagged edge tore into the flesh of the victim and increased the bleeding and bruising.

The soldiers stripped Jesus naked and tied him to a post, his arms stretched upward and secured by ropes at the wrist. Two soldiers scourged him, one tall and one short, to make sure the whole back of Christ's body would be reached with maximum force. The legal limit of lashes was thirty-nine. We do not know if they exceeded this limit. Sometimes this happened, as is evident from the Shroud of Turin, where the imprint of a crucified man shows that the victim received at least sixty lashes.

For many centuries countless Christians have contemplated this scene. Their meditation transcends any morbid fascination with physical punishment. A stream of Christian poetry and hymns reflect the faith insights that are drawn from this experience. The sick, the lonely, the crushed and the poor identify with this agony of Jesus, because he has chosen to share in their own pain. The scene convinces them that God now knows what they suffer because, in his

Son, he experiences human suffering and humiliation. This God is no bystander in the face of human pain. This God is truly compassionate in that basic meaning of that word — one who visibly "suffers with" (*cumpassio* in the Latin).

A second truth drawn from this meditation is that salvation is experienced in the wounds of Christ. Isaiah already gained this insight centuries ago. "He was wounded for our transgressions, he was bruised for our iniquities. Upon him was the chastisement that made us whole. With his stripes (lashes) we are healed" (Is. 53:5, RSV). Our suffering is overcome by Christ's suffering. Our wounds are healed by Christ's wounds, not necessarily through miraculous cures but by the gift of faith Jesus offers, a faith that involves pain in the goal of liberation from sin. When Isaiah says that by the wounds of the Suffering Servant we are healed, he is ultimately talking about theological healing, the cleansing away of our sins.

That is one side of the healing work of Jesus in his being scourged. He liberates us *from* our sins, but also liberates for inner freedom and personal dignity. To gaze on him at the whipping post, we ponder the externals of indignity, degradation, the appalling result of his persecutors' perversity, inhumanity, and total insensitivity. There's nothing pleasant about the event. Flesh ripped, blue welts erupting, sweat from the heat of pain and the sun, dehydration and thirst, unimaginable stabs of pain, helplessness, the shame of one's nude body exposed to the eyes of men and women. We cannot ignore the smell of blood, the grunts of the scourgers, the sound of the whip.

The point of forcing ourselves to face the grisly reality of the scourging is to see through the human indignity Jesus shows us on the surface. With our faith we penetrate the interior world of Jesus. There we experience with awe the inner drama of Christ, his extraordinary dignity despite outward appearances, his ability to look dehumanized and yet radiate the magnificence of the glory-presence of the Word as well as the splendor of being human.

We experience the flow of salvation from his center of power and grace, liberation from sin, liberation for the practice of every value and virtue that will be the true source of human dignity. He is saving us from pride, greed, lust and all the other self destructive forces in our souls. He is saving us for humility, generosity, chaste living and all the other spiritual powers that make us noble and worthwhile. Not for one moment is he a pawn of fate, a helpless human set adrift on the ash heap of history. At his core is his freedom, at once human and divine which no diabolical force or other human resource can dislodge. From that center under the noise of the action at the whipping post he reaches out to the center in every one of us. He thirsts to unite us in the best of all solidarities, the communion of Love that no other power can overcome.

We should hold firmly to our focus on the inner center of Jesus even as we watch the outward indignities multiply and produce a dreadful cumulative physical and emotional effect. After scourging Jesus, the soldiers made a crown of thorns (actually a cap) and draped him in a purple cloak and mocked him. "Hail, King of the Jews!" (verse 3). Soldiers often played this game of the king, but usually seldom so cruelly, for normally the crown was made of paper, a fool's crown for a dunce. They sought comic relief from their deadly duty. Here, the reality of blood lust overcame their more civil impulses.

A pile of thorn branches would be nearby for making fires on the cool nights. Quite possibly the gritty thorn fronds of the date palms were at hand. If so, the contrast of Sunday's palms of glory with Friday's palms of pain provides its own message. The skull bleeds easily and profusely. The cap of thorns would be secured by some heavy beating of the head. The old hymn is correct when it says, "O sacred head surrounded with crown of piercing thorn."

And so the soldiers knelt before the King of Glory. They bowed in mockery little knowing they bent with a gesture of reverence before the Master of the universe . The heartless prostrated before the King of hearts. They saw nothing more than a helpless man whom they could beat up and make fun of.

Jesus stood there, his body smarting with waves of pain, his head a blinding headache, all his natural sensitivities open to resentment at being treated both as a fool and a human rag doll. Yet incredibly his glory radiated there even more powerfully than in the excitement of the miracles of the Bread, Wine, and Raising of Lazarus. No enthusiastic crowds sing his praises. But angels worship him and praise God for the shimmering radiance they behold at his center. He looks like a broken man to some. To our eyes of faith, he manifests his expansive inner power, becoming more majestic even as outward details tell us otherwise.

His center glows with resolve, shines with love, pulses with forgiveness, expands with the confidence that evil's kingdom is about to meet defeat. He will have one shattering moment ahead when he shouts his cry of abandonment from the cross (see Mt. 27:46). Yet even in that seemingly shaky moment, he will testify that he has completed the descent from the heavenly realms, the kenosis-self-emptying. Only complete ascent and glory will assuredly follow.

Scene Five: Behold the Man (Outside). Pilate brought Jesus outside, hoping his pathetic beaten appearance would be enough to persuade them to let him go free. For a second time, Pilate publicly said he found no guilt in Jesus. No capital crime. Therefore, there should be no capital punishment. Pilate pointed at Jesus and said, "Behold, the man" (verse 5).

Pilate's words possessed a meaning far deeper than he meant and one more profound than was appreciated by the crowd. Pilate had first called Jesus a king. Now he calls him a man. What he did not realize was that all the royalty of the truly human, all that really is human, was embodied in Jesus. Just when he looked his worst as a human being, Jesus was presented to the world as "the man," a real human being in full dignity. This insight was captured wonderfully by the Second Vatican Council, which we paraphrase here.

It is only in the mystery of the Word made flesh that the mystery of the human becomes clear. Christ fully reveals what it means to be human and brings to light our most high calling. Jesus, the image of the invisible God, was a fully realized human being. He restored each of us to the likeness of God that was distorted by sin. Humanity, by the very fact that it was assumed — not absorbed — by him, has been raised in us to a dignity beyond compare. (Read and meditate on all of paragraph 22 in "Church in the Modern World."[*]).

In Matthew's gospel (25:35-45), Jesus said believers would recognize him among the hungry, the thirsty, the strangers, the naked, the imprisoned. His most powerful presence would be noticed among the poorest of the poor, the oppressed, the homeless, the despised, the weak, the lonely, the forgotten, the so-called "uglies"

---

[*] "The Church in the Modern World," *Gaudium et spes*, *Vatican Council II: Conciliar and Post Conciliar Documents*, Austin Flannery, ed. (Northport, NY: Costello Publishing Co., 1981).

of this world. Look at Jesus in this scene. Thirsty from loss of fluids, imprisoned, a stranger's purple cloak covering his nakedness, hungry, in pain, a stranger in the Antonia, despised. He lived in that moment the very traits he described in Matthew. We are called upon to recognize the real Jesus in such a state. Let us see in him the precious gift of humanity that no disfigurement, deprivation, or social downfall can hide. Behold the Jesus who reveals what is genuinely human to every human being.

A force of evil overtook that little gathering of respectable citizens, religious leaders, and guards. The assembly became a mob. Sin possessed their hearts and perverted their capacity to recognize a just, honest, loving and innocent Jesus. Just as tragic, they fail to recognize or respect the human dignity of the man they see before them. They allow their voices to ring with shouts, "Crucify him, crucify him!" (verse 6). The voice of compassion for his wounded humanity is missing. One listens in vain for the sound of faith in the warm and healing Word of God become flesh. No reason. No faith. Just emotion, blind prejudice and the protective justification that Jesus broke their law by claiming to be the Son of God. They took their most sacred possession, the Holy Scripture, and used it as an instrument to bring about judicial murder. They used the word of God to kill the Word of God.

Scene Six: The Uses of Power (Inside). Pilate and Jesus go back into the residence. The governor became "more afraid" (verse 8). He had two kinds of fear, one caused by the dissidents who were not backing down and beginning to threaten him, the other a superstitious fear of Jesus who might be some kind of divinity. After all the mob spoke of him as a Son of God. Fear would both drive out any positive step Pilate might have taken, and trigger his survival instincts. Whatever tiny grain of humanitarian instincts he may have felt would soon yield to his customary political ones.

Peering deeply at Jesus, Pilate asked him where he came from. Jesus remained silent. His silence was meant to provoke Pilate to reflect upon himself. He must now come to his own decisions. Jesus had offered him the possibility of change, but Christ would not force the governor to change.

Impatiently, Pilate raised the question of power. This was a subject dear to his heart, one with which he was totally familiar. He indicated that he could simply use his political power to save him.

Jesus evaded his political statement. Jesus had never made politics a major element in his teachings, miracles or witnessing of the kingdom. He simply told Pilate that whatever power the governor possessed, it came from above.

Scene Seven: A Fatal Judgment (Outside). Still, uncharacteristically, Pilate made one more effort to release Jesus, but caved in before the taunts of the crowd that he was not a loyal public servant of Caesar's. He could hardly be so if he was willing to let a rival king go free. The mood had turned as ugly as it could get. Pilate sat on his judgement chair, placed Jesus on the stone pavement and said, "Behold, your king" (verse 14). Refer here to what was said above about Christ's royal humanity. Above the crescendo of the yelling mob, Pilate heard the priests say they had no king but Caesar. Their faith told them that only God is their king. Their politics taught them that kingship belonged to the House of David. Their emotions persuaded them to shout allegiance to the half mad emperor Tiberias wandering about his palace at Capri.

Pilate handed Jesus over to be crucified.

It was noon.

The priests at the temple had begun the sacrifice of the lambs.

The people had begun to sing the holy texts of the Haggadah.

At the beginning of this gospel, John the Baptist pointed to Jesus and called him God's lamb. The sacrifice of the Passover lambs at the temple will be matched by the sacrifice of the Lamb of God who marches to the cross to save us from our sins.

The Crucifixion (Jn. 19:17-22)

The Persians invented crucifixion. The Romans adopted it for executions in their provinces. The victim carried the cross-bar to the place of execution where a vertical post was prepared to receive the cross-bar. The prisoner was mounted on the cross either with ropes or with nails. We know Jesus was nailed to the cross. Thomas the apostle said he would not believe in Christ's resurrection unless he could see the nail marks and put his fingers into the spaces left by them. Jesus obliged Thomas during an Easter appearance and invited him to do what he wished (see Jn. 20:24-27).

Crucified victims died from asphyxiation, a process that could take as long as a week. The downward pull of gravity weakened their arms to the point where they could no longer lift themselves up to exhale their breath. The execution mound was a few feet above ground level, hence relatives and friends could easily converse with the victim during the dying process. All observers agree that crucifixion was a horrible and painful way to die.

In John's account Jesus carries the cross-bar by himself to Calvary. Matthew says that Simon of Cyrene helped him with it (Mt. 27:32). Calvary means place of the skull. Some have concluded that this meant the area was used for beheadings. A legend says that Adam was buried there, thus connecting the death of Jesus with that of Adam. Hence, in a vivid manner the saving blood of the new Adam (Jesus) would flow upon the old Adam.

Two others were crucified with Jesus, one on each side of him. Pilate ordered an inscription to be placed over the head of Jesus. It read, "Jesus the Nazorean, King of the Jews." It was written in three languages, Roman, Greek, and Hebrew. The leading priests asked Pilate to change the wording to "He said he was King of the Jews." Pilate tired of their pressure and stubbornly left the words as they were.

Woman, Behold, Your Son (Jn. 19:23-27)

Four men stood guard at the cross. They divided Christ's clothing among themselves. This would have included a tunic, belt, sandals and head covering. They gambled for his fifth piece of apparel, his seamless robe. Customarily, a high priest wore a seamless robe, hence that fact of Jesus owning one assumed a special symbolism for he became the high priest of the new covenant.

Since the beginning of his *kenosis* (this Greek word means emptying) he progressively emptied himself of any trace of the status of heavenly glory. During his journey on earth he gradually let go also of all earthly possession. He left behind his modest, comfortable home in Nazareth. He let go of his trade as a carpenter. As a wandering preacher, he depended on the hospitality of others. Little by little his life exhibited the utmost simplicity. Now at the end of his life, the few pieces of clothing he owned were taken away from him. Possibly his robe had been woven by his mother. Son and mother watched the robe go to a guard who won a bet. The long process of emptying was reaching its conclusion. What is emptied of all possessiveness will be filled with the eternally satisfying life of God.

As Mary's only son, Jesus had some unfinished business. He asked John to look after his mother and take care of her. "Behold, your mother" (verse 27). John welcomed this responsibility and took her into his household. Tradition says that John and Mary moved to Ephesus, a city of 250,000 people, nestled in a valley with mountain walls on three sides and a canal-port that connected the city to the Mediterranean. Today one may visit the House of Mary a mile above the city.

Jesus turned to Mary and said, "Woman, behold, your son" (verse 26). This is the second time in John's gospel he addresses her as "woman." At Cana he addressed her as woman to indicate her elevation to a spiritual role in the unfolding of God's plan of salvation. He had told her then that his "hour" had not yet come. Clearly, the hour had finally arrived and she would be intimately united to the event at the cross. He spoke of her as mother when entrusting her to John. That was his filial responsibility to her as his mother.

At Calvary he addressed her as woman who is called to be the mother of Christians, the mother of the church. By saying, "Behold, your son," Jesus extends her motherhood beyond John to all women and men in the church. It is said that dying people need the permission of loved ones to enter death. They need to be released by those who mean the most to them. Jesus was asking her to release him with all the love and generosity she had shown from the joyful Annunciation to this tragic moment. Just as he has accepted in peace this forthcoming death, so must she.

She must let go of the physical body of Jesus. She will gain the Mystical Body of her Son. As Jesus requested her permission to go into death, he also asked her to deepen her faith and love more than she would have imagined up to that point. He also wanted her to say a "yes" (a fiat in Latin) to sharing in the growth of the Mystical Body just as she had agreed to his physical birth at the Annunciation. At Bethlehem she bore Jesus with all the beauty of a Christmas carol. At Calvary she faced the challenge of being the mother of Christians with all the sorrow of a death watch. Yet the outcome is so different. All she could find was a stable at Bethlehem. Now she had the whole world to work in. She surrendered to God's will when Gabriel asked her to be the mother of Jesus. She surrendered to the will of the Son of God — her Son, too, for she is the God bearer (*Theotokos*) — when he asked her to be the mother of Christians.

At the Annunciation Gabriel sang the first Ave Maria.

Today, in perfect harmony with Gabriel we add, Salve Regina!

I Thirst . . . It Is finished (Jn. 19:28-30)

By now the body of Jesus was heavily dehydrated. Loss of bodily fluids, blood from the beatings and water from the sun, heat and exertion, led him to cry out, "I thirst" (verse 28). That was the physical cause of his words. However, at this moment in his passion, he had a far deeper concern, one related to his saving mission that was entering its final minutes at Calvary. He was asking those who heard him, and we who hear him now, to be open to his love and forgiveness. "Let me love you. Let me forgive you."

His thirst was fundamentally spiritual, an enormous desire to share the love he had come to earth to share with everyone. Many people on their deathbeds say they wish they had loved more during their lives. On his deathbed, Jesus said he wished more had accepted the love he generously offered every day of his life. The risen Jesus continues to speak his "I thirst" in the world today. For all those who feel unloved, he offers a fulfilling love. Acceptance of his love is the key.

Nearby was a jug of soldier's wine. They used it to numb their own feelings as well as to quell the pain of the crucified. A guard put some wine on a sponge and offered it to Jesus. When Jesus had taken the wine, he said, "It is finished" (verse 30). Jesus had considered his passion as an act of worship. He stretched to the limit his calling as high priest of the new covenant. He reached back into the sacred history of his people and wove all their forms of worship into a seamless robe of holy adoration, obedience, and praise.

He took the "olah," the holocaust of a lamb by Abel and made a total offering of himself. He seized the cup of wine that Melchisedech used as a libation — pouring off the wine onto a rock as a toast of thanksgiving to God — and poured out fully the wine of his blood as thanks for the reality of salvation for all. He picked up the twelve loaves at the temple altar and turned himself into the bread to be broken for the redemption of the world.

Jesus gathered into his heart all those who had assembled for the friendship meal of Passover and created the new Passover, the

Eucharist which would continue the effects of his passion and resurrection into history. He brought the scapegoat of the feast of Atonement out of the wilderness and made himself the one upon whom all the sins of the world would be heaped. Just when he seemed most separated from every creature on earth, he was witnessing solidarity with everyone, atonement, at-one-ment.

It was three in the afternoon.

At the temple the priest offered the last lamb.

He said "Kalah," which means "It is finished."

At Calvary Jesus offered himself as the true lamb of God.

He said, "Kalah," which means, "It is finished."

The Piercing of Christ's Side (Jn. 19:31-37)

The Jews had a rule that all dead bodies should be buried before Passover. The two thieves were still alive. Soldiers took mallets and broke their legs. The shock hastened their death. Jesus was already dead, but a soldier took a knife and pierced his heart as a kind of assurance. The bones of Passover lambs were not to be broken, so neither would Christ's bones be touched. Water and blood flowed from Christ's side. This event was a sign of the birth of the church. On the cross the church was born in the water of baptism and the blood of the Eucharist.

The Burial of Jesus (Jn. 19:38-42)

Christian art has supplied the scene of the descent from the cross and Mary's claim of the body of her son. Michelangelo's Pieta best expressed the tone and mood of John's gospel. He sculptured fulfillment, achievement, glory muted by tranquility. The nail holes in Christ's hands and feet are tiny holes. Violence has vanished and Jesus sleeps peacefully in Mary's arms. Jesus radiates sympathy for those who stand before this scene in which he lay in his mother's lap. We behold the sublimity of Jesus and Mary. Their harmony reflects the reconciliation of nature, people, and God just accomplished. Christ's divinity quietly emerges through his exquisite humanity. We look at Mary's face, like that of a maiden, filled with silent composure. The beauty of the two figures keeps revealing the grandeur of their inner lives.

It is time for the burial. Jesus had once said it would be harder for a rich man to get into heaven than for a camel to squeeze through the eye of a needle. Two rich men came forward from the anonymity of the crowd at Calvary. They had been secret admirers of Jesus. Joseph of Arimathea claimed Christ's body from Pilate and then donated his new tomb in the garden next to Calvary. Nicodemus, who had visited Jesus at night long ago to discuss his teachings, brought one hundred pounds of spices to anoint the body.

Joseph's tomb was carved out of a rock. A flagstone was placed there for anointing the body. The gift of Nicodemus was enough for a royal anointing. After Christ's body was wrapped in a shroud, it was placed on a ledge. Mary and the mourners took one last look. It was evening. They withdrew from the chamber and rolled a stone against the door of the tomb. Their final traditional prayer was, "Dust you are and unto dust you will return" (See Gn. 3:19).

In three days Jesus would conquer this death and transform that humble dust into the glory of a risen body.

St. Francis loved to meditate on the passion. He would sing about it, simulating the movement of a bow across a violin. Then his exuberance would dissolve in tears for Jesus. On his own death bed, he received the stigmata, the wounds of Jesus. He died with a psalm on his lips.

Reflection

1. What spontaneous reactions do I have as I visualize the scourging of Jesus?
2. Why do the poor, the suffering, and the lonely find that meditating on the wounds of Jesus consoles them?
3. Jesus saves me from sin. He also liberates me to practice Christian values and virtues. How does this affect me?
4. What reflection can I offer to others about the crowning with thorns?
5. Why is Vatican II able to say Jesus reveals what is truly human to every human being?
6. How successful have I been in practicing "the discovery of Jesus" in the hungry, naked, lonely, and obsessed?
7. Jesus asked Mary to be our spiritual mother. How has my relation to Mary developed over the years?

8. Jesus thirsts for us to accept his love and forgiveness. How attentive have I been to his offer?
9. What artistic image or poetic description of the crucifixion touches me the most?
10. What moment in the passion narrative moves me the most deeply?

Prayer

Jesus, my savior, I thank you for the love you showed for me and all the world in your blessed passion and death. I adore you for your willingness to undergo injustice, rejection, pain and death that I might be liberated from my sins. I praise you for liberating me for a life of Christian virtues which witness your presence in the world and assures the best human fulfillment. Keep me ever near you.

20 I Found Him Whom My Heart Loves

Love Made John Believe (Jn. 20:1-9)

Dawn, Sunday morning.

Mary Magdalene came to the tomb and saw that the stone was rolled away. Christ's body was missing. Immediately, she ran back and reported this to Peter and John.

Peter and John ran to the tomb. John arrived first but did not enter the burial chamber. Peter came and entered the grave room. He saw the shroud rolled up on the shelf where Christ's body had been laid. The cloth which had covered his head was in a separate place. The body was gone.

John saw this and believed. What led him to faith? Did he conclude the body would not have been stolen because robbers would scarcely have taken the time to unwrap the body and carry away a nude, stiff corpse? John Chrysostom points out the unlikelihood of theft. "If anyone had removed the body, he would not have stripped it first. Nor would he have taken the trouble to roll up the head covering and put it in a place by itself" (*Homily* 85, 4).

The apostle John may have deduced that the body was not stolen, but love is the real explanation of his faith. Love is the best road to faith. John was the disciple whom Jesus loved. John welcomed and returned Christ's love. John alone of the apostles stood at the cross. It was to John that Jesus entrusted his mother.

Later Jesus would tell Thomas that seeing his body in order to come to faith was not as great as believing without seeing. Possibly Jesus looked at John when saying these words to Thomas. However, the key insight here is that it was the power of John's love for Jesus that enabled him to believe in the resurrection. In this gospel account, the disciple who was bound closest in love to Jesus was the fastest to look for him and the first to believe in him.

Jesus Calls Magdalene to Faith (Jn. 20:11-18)

The story of another great lover of Jesus, Mary Magdalene, follows immediately. The process of how love brought her to faith is described in greater detail and introduces the normal biblical dialogue for faith events — a divine call and a human response. On that Easter morning, Magdalene lived out the description of a lover seeking the beloved as recounted in the Song of Songs.

I will seek whom my heart loves. . .
The watchmen came upon me as they made their
rounds of the city:
Have you seen him whom my heart loves?
I had hardly left them when I found him whom my heart loves.
I took hold of him and would not let him go.

—Song of Songs 3:2-4

This text illustrates the drive of the lover to union with, presence to and possession of the beloved. Magdalene embodied this description perfectly. She had returned to the tomb and remained outside it weeping. She peered inside the chamber and saw two angels in white sitting on the grave bench. They asked her why she was weeping. She told them that someone had taken away the body of Jesus and she did not know where it was. At that moment she heard someone come up to the tomb. It was Jesus. But she did not recognize him.

The Easter narratives stress that the risen Jesus is often not recognized at first when he is encountered. The two disciples on the road to Emmaus failed to know him in the beginning. The apostles at Christ's lake-side appearance did not recognize him. Mary Magdalene thought he was a gardener.

Why is this so? For one thing, it teaches that Christ's followers were not credulously expecting his resurrection.

Second, it demonstrates that Christ's resurrected body was different from his historical body. St. Paul explained this to the Corinthians. "So also is the resurrection of the dead. It is sown corruptible; it is raised incorruptible. . . . It is sown weak; it is raised powerful. It is sown a natural body; it is raised a spiritual body" (I Cor. 15:42-44). Nonetheless, we have the same Jesus. The Christ of Galilee and Judea is the same Jesus after the resurrection, but his body is different — transformed, spiritual, glorified.

Last, just as it took faith to really know who was the Jesus of

Nazareth, Capernaum and Jerusalem, so it will still require faith to recognize him in his risen state.

Jesus asked Magdalene why she was crying. Thinking he was the gardener, she asked him if he knew what happened to Christ's body. She would go and get it. Jesus said, "Mary." She replied, "Rabbouni," which means teacher. The process that led to Magdalene's recognition of Jesus involved four stages. (l). Jesus sought her out. (2). Mary was a seeker after Jesus. (3). The Master called her by name, (4). Mary responded in faith. This is the typical description of the four major steps in the faith journey in Scripture. God in search of humans. The human heart questing God. The call from God. The human response in faith.

The Emmaus disciples only recognized Jesus after the breaking of the bread. Mary only recognized Jesus after the "breaking" of the Word. Thus Jesus shows us the twofold ministry of his risen life — Sacrament and Word.

With the enthusiasm of love, Magdalene clung to Jesus. The Master gently said that she must let go of him. He must complete his saving work by going to the Father and send the Holy Spirit. He was not against her touching him, else why would he have invited Thomas to touch the wounds in his hands and side? Magdalene had misunderstood his presence in the garden as his permanent presence. Jesus honored her by confiding in her that his permanent presence to her and all believers would be by the Holy Spirit.

Jesus approved her magnificent desire, her longing to be close to him, to possess her beloved, but he helped her see how it would be truly fulfilled. "Not yet," said Jesus. She must go to the apostles with his message and prepare them for his permanent presence in the Spirit. He made her an evangelizer of the Good News to the apostolic college. That is why the Christians of the Middle Ages praised Magdalene as the "Apostola apostolorum," the apostle to the apostles. That is why the next scene shows him breathing out the gift of the Spirit to the apostles. Magdalene prepared them for this gift.

Jesus Gives the Spirit to the Apostles (Jn. 20:19-23)

Easter night.

The eleven apostles had returned to the Upper Room and locked the doors for fear of those Jews who had been involved in the crucifixion of Jesus. Thomas, however, had left earlier in the evening. Suddenly, Jesus appeared to them and said, "Peace be with you" (verse 19). At the Last Supper Jesus had shared his peace with them and told them to let go of their fear. He had promised to return to them and has now proved it.

He showed them the wound marks in his hands and his side. Joy overwhelmed them as they recognized the Lord. He then gave them the commission to continue his work in the world. "As the Father has sent me, so I send you" (verse 21). Jesus depended on them and the Christian community to take his Good News to all the earth. At the same time, they will need the message, power and authority of Jesus to carry out such a mission. The Christian community depends on Jesus for its success.

Lastly, their mission must be similar to that of Jesus. As the Father had sent Jesus, so Christ sends them. As Jesus had obeyed the Father and represented him faithfully, so must the apostles and the Christian community obey Jesus and represent him faithfully. There can be no other message than that of Jesus. There can be no other name than that of Jesus to be preached.

Then Jesus breathed on them and gave them the Holy Spirit. He accompanied this with words about the forgiving of sins. God the Father had breathed into Adam the breath of human life. Now Jesus breathed into the apostles the breath of the Holy Spirit, a divine life. Jesus conferred on the apostles the power of forgiving sins. They in turn pass on that power to others through ordination.

This brief scene is filled with truth. It reveals the fulfillment of the promise of the messiah. Jesus had come to save us from our sins and to give us a new life that will enable us to reach the fullness of humanity by the creative power of the Spirit. Risen from the dead, Jesus wears the marks of the cross to remind us that his passion and death were conditions for the gifts of love he now shares with us. The forgiveness of our sins is a grace, a costly grace. Risen, he convinces us that death can be overcome. Commissioning the apostles, he assures us that our sins are forgivable. Breathing on them, he excites us with the promise of personal fulfillment in its most positive sense, spiritual as well as in other ways.

Thomas, Do Not Be Unbelieving, But Believing (Jn. 20:-31)

When Thomas returned, the apostles told him the exciting news about the resurrection of Jesus. He protested that he would not believe unless he could see Jesus and put his finger into the nail marks and his hand into Jesus's side. The following Sunday night he was given the chance to do this. Jesus appeared again, once more said "Peace" and then invited Thomas to touch his wounds. "Do not be unbelieving, but believe" (verse 27). The text does not say whether Thomas actually inspected Christ's wounds in this way. Apparently, Christ's inviting word was enough. Thomas replied with these beautiful words of faith. "My Lord and my God" (verse 28). Jesus then commented that the people who have not seen and believed are truly blessed.

In some ways Thomas seems very modern in his doubt and pessimism. The comedian, Woody Allen, has made his reputation by making jokes out of popular questioning of all traditional values. "How is it possible to find meaning in a finite world, given my waist and shirt size?... Can technology really be the answer to it all when my toaster hasn't worked properly in four years."

The contemporary form of doubting is questioning. One must distinguish between good questioning and bad. Good questioning involves an honest curiosity about life, a quest for facts and truth. It embraces the attitude of wonder which is the capacity to see beneath the surface of things. Good questioning is the soul of philosophy, science, and scholarship.

Bad questioning is a veiled attack on cherished values. It is a hidden agenda for cynicism. It is a cover-up for pessimism. This kind of questioning sounds innocent, but underneath it is a negative attitude. It reminds one of the proverb, "A fool can ask more questions than a wise man can answer." Instead of being a sincere search for truth, it really challenges the credibility of the truthsayer.

Is doubting a problem for Christians today? Yes, for some of them. They veil their doubts in the fashionable, socially acceptable cloud of questions. They sound like they have a heartfelt desire for truth, but in reality they mask a cynicism about moral values and the truth claims of Jesus. But there are also Christians who have sincere doubts and raise questions that reveal their heartfelt search for God. They are truly seekers. With time, grace, patience and love, they will receive God's reassuring response.

As we said, Thomas sounds very modern. He might easily say today, "I have serious reservations about your statements, dear brother apostles. Are you certain you saw Jesus? You don't think you are suffering from a bad case of wish fulfillment? Perhaps you were trying to force your dreams to come true? I want to believe you. Help me get at what you evidently experienced."

In other words Thomas was an honest broker. He did not have a closed mind. He was willing to listen, to probe and be open to the possibility they shared with him. He is intrigued by their news, but ever the cautious man who realizes truth is not won easily. He is an example of the wholesome questioning practiced today. It proved he was a seeker after truth. He sought and he found. He met Jesus and worshiped him. "My Lord and my God!"

I have to question, Thomas said.
That's my way.
Kill my question and I'll be dead.
It's my say.
Jesus the answer entered the room.
Touch me now.
In his heart deep faith did loom.
My Lord, Wow!

Reflection

1. How does my love for Jesus help me to have a stronger faith in him?
2. If I had been there Easter morning with Peter and John and seen the empty tomb, what might have been my reaction?
3. Review the steps that led to Mary's recognition of the risen Jesus. What faith experiences in my life have corresponded to these steps?
4. What are the three purposes of the "non-recognition" stories in the gospels? How are they relevant to my faith growth?
5. Magdalene wanted to hold onto Jesus who counseled her to let go. What are aspects of my faith life that I must let go?
6. What are some experiences in my life in which I felt the peace of Christ?
7. I received a special gift of the Holy Spirit at my Confirmation. What impact does that experience have on me now?
8. Jesus empowered the apostles to be ministers of the Sacrament of Reconciliation. What influence does this sacrament have on my life?

9. In what ways do I find I am like Thomas the doubter?
10. How do I handle the faith problems of other people?

Prayer

Alleluia! Praise be to you, Lord Jesus, risen from the dead. You responded to the love of John and Magdalene with your self revelation. You gifted the apostles with the Spirit and the power to forgive sins. Increase my faith, forgive my sins, and fill me with your Spirit.

21 Happy Ending

Most people like a happy ending to a story. Sometimes they want to change existing classics which have tragic conclusions so that they end happily. Oxford professor John Barton points out that in the eighteenth century the tragedy of King Lear was changed so that Lear was restored to the throne. The same was true in Handel's oratorio about Jephtha's daughter, who in the Bible met a sorrowful end. Handel introduced a divine intervention so that the girl's life would be saved after all.

In modern times there seems to be more willingness to confront despair. So we want the story to end that way if it is supposed to. We do not like "improvements" to such stories because we feel such happy endings are not really endings at all, but mere appendages. We do not prefer characters who suffer in Shakespeare and the Bible to live by different principles than those in real life.

We Christians view the events of Christ's life, death, and resurrection as the greatest drama of all time. We dislike a facile happy ending to the story as though God were a magician who waved a magic wand and wiped away all of Christ's pain with a brand new life. That is why the Easter stories insist that Jesus wore the marks of his passion in his risen life.

Moreover, Christ's resurrection is not tacked onto the passion story like a pleasant addition. Nor is it simply a delicious surprise nor a fascinating unusual fact such as Australian Koala's never drink water — just the alcoholic juice of the Eucalyptus leaf. The faith statement that Jesus rose from the dead never to die again means we have a different kind of story. We have it on God's word that the life and death of Jesus was not the result of random historical forces, but part of an eternal plan for our salvation. God is the author of this drama. Hence the Gospel is not a tragedy but a story with a real happy ending that is consistent with the life and death of Jesus.

John's gospel especially contains this insight. The moment of Christ's death is already a moment of glory. Easter so illumines the suffering that went before it that the very cross itself is a pool of light. This theme is beautifully remembered in a text from the liturgy of the Eastern Church. "Since it brings life, the tomb of Jesus is lovelier indeed than paradise. It is the fountain from which our resurrection springs." St. John is so taken with the Easter joy that rings beyond the walls of this world that he devotes two full chapters to the resurrection appearances. We have seen the first one. We proceed now to look at his last chapter.

The Lakeside Appearance (Jn. 21:1-14)

The scene is the Galilean lakeside, the site so filled with the joyous memories of the beginning of Christ's ministry. Seven of Christ's disciples joined Peter on a fishing trip. They fished all night and caught nothing. At dawn they returned to shore and saw a man standing on the beach. He asked them if they caught anything. They said, "No." The man told them to cast their net one more time on the right side of the boat — the lucky side — and they will catch fish.

They followed his advice and could scarcely bring in their net because it was overloaded with fish. This event is similar to the other abundant gifts in John: wine at Cana, bread on the mountain, living water at Tabernacles, eternal life from the Good Shepherd and the outpouring of the Spirit. John then realized, "It is the Lord!" (verse 7). This so excited Peter that he jumped out of the boat and waded to shore to meet Jesus. The others brought their catch of 153 fish to the beach. The fish symbolize the great numbers who will be brought into the Christian community. St. Jerome stated that it was commonly held in New Testament times that the lake had 153 species of fish, though his source has never been found. Still, his conclusion is valid, namely, that the Gospel would be preached to every imaginable type of person in the world.

Jesus had brought bread and lit a charcoal fire. "Come and have breakfast," he said. Christ's meal reminded them of the loaves miracle and the giving of the Spirit. This event was another faith testimony to the reality of the resurrection. The gospels present a risen Jesus who could be felt, touched, seen, heard, eat bread and fish, make a charcoal fire, walk, talk, give instruction, argue, overcome doubt — and insist he was not a ghost.

The cumulative effect of the numerous resurrection narratives is that Jesus was truly, really, physically present to the disciples in his appearances. The "non-recognition stories" affirm the new spiritual quality of his risen body. The "recognition" stories just as strongly affirm the realism of his appearances and the certainty of the witnesses. The risen Jesus of the gospel narratives is robust, realistic, credible, involved and practical enough to cook breakfast.

Your risen body, Lord, I do behold
Alleluia!
This day must all the world be told.
Alleluia!
Love has beaten death.
Given us the Spirit's breath.

Do You Love Me, Peter? (Jn. 21:15-19)

After breakfast Jesus asked Peter if he loved him more than all the others. "Yes, Lord, you know I love you." Jesus commissioned him to feed his lambs. Jesus repeated the question again. Peter once more affirmed his love and was told to feed Christ's sheep. A third time Jesus asked Peter if he loved him more than anyone else. Distressed that Jesus seemed not to believe him, he complained that Jesus knew everything. He certainly knew that he was loved by Peter. "Feed my sheep," replied Christ.

Peter's public declarations of love put behind him once and for all his triple denial during the passion. Seldom have we heard of a more touching call to leadership. Here is a vision of leadership that is founded on love and affection between the leader and Jesus — and between the leader and his potential followers. This "love model" of leadership balances the "institutional model" of leadership seen at Caesarea Philipi where Jesus made Peter the rock upon which his church would be built (see Mt. 16:13-20). The total ministry of Peter would embrace his call as Rock and as Lover.

The Easter scene at the beach discloses a vision of leadership that flows from an adult view of loving union, trust, and respect. Jesus took a public risk to ask Peter for love's vows. Jesus did not first ask for apologies about the denial. He simply voiced a candid appeal for affection. Peter caught the precise dignity of the moment, the fresh opportunity to be born again. He put behind him his failures and disappointments. He did his weeping and confessed his sins.

This Easter dawn at the beach where Peter had launched so many fishing trips — his homeland of Galilee — signaled the beginning of a new creation, a new Peter who sang out unabashedly of his love for Jesus.

He would never be a St. John taking spiritual flights like an eagle. He could not dream of matching the eloquence or literary genius of St. Paul. He had a humbler form of genius, the capacity to become the first chief shepherd of the church. He remained lovingly faithful to Jesus until his martyrdom in the circus of Nero some thirty years later. Michelangelo has memorialized the dual qualities of leadership in Peter at the base of the great dome in St. Peter's basilica in Rome. Inscribed there is the "Rock" text from Matthew and the "Love" text from John. Jesus knew his man and was not disappointed by his choice.

The Disciple Jesus Loved (Jn. 21:20-25)

The disciple whom Jesus loved was John the son of Zebedee, the brother of James and an apostle. Tradition says he moved to Ephesus with the Mother of Jesus and that he lived to the age of 94, which may account for the verse in this section that states he would live until the Second Coming of Jesus (verse 22). He died a natural death and not as a martyr like the other apostles.

St. John is best known as the apostle of love, as can be seen in the tone and mood he set in writing this gospel and his three New Testament letters. He wrote from experience, especially as the best friend of Jesus. He was not only capable of loving Jesus, but of being loved by him. In true love, one must be willing to be loved as well as to love.

It may seem remarkable that the Son of God was able to have a personal friend he seemed to like and love more than others. We might imagine that Jesus would have loved everyone with equal affection, or that he at least loved people with the same intimacy they showed to him. Yet Jesus shows himself to be entirely human in his feelings and desires. There is nothing contrary to the Gospel spirit in this.

Some argue that Christian love is supposed to be so all embracing that it is shared equally with everyone. But the best preparation for loving everyone is to develop intimate friendship with those who are near us. We begin by loving our friends who are close to us, then we expand the circle of our affections until they reach out to everyone. If we begin to try to love everyone first, our effort will be little more than an abstraction, like the idealist who loved the world, but could not stand people. Loving all men and women means being positively disposed to them and being ready to help should they come our way.

Love is a habit which demands practice. We cannot practice on the whole human race, but we can practice on the people in our circle of acquaintances. We accede to their wishes even when contrary to our own. We share their burdens and respond to their faults with kindness and a forgiving attitude. We note their good points and try to imitate them. Quietly, over a long period, we root love in our hearts and slowly cultivate the tree of affection.

This is the special gift of St. John as beloved disciple of Jesus. He is a mirror that shows us such an attractive and appealing quality in Jesus, the value of making deep and lasting friends with the people at hand. In finding John to be such a good personal friend, Jesus did what we all can do, practice friendship with a few so as to give love to the many.

John concludes his gospel by telling us that what he wrote is the truth and that there was so much more to write that "I do not think the whole world would contain the books that would be written" (verse 25).

We began this commentary by listening to the singing of the community of St. John the Beloved in Ephesus. They chanted praise to the Word become flesh. We close with the same scene, this time allowing the lens of our mind to focus on the old apostle thinking of the best friendship he ever had. We have witnessed the great affection that existed between him and the apostles and the privileged blessing of having the Holy Mother of Jesus in his home, radiating faith and prayer while he wrote his extraordinary gospel.

The singing has now stopped and the 90-year-old apostle begins another message to his community —

Beloved, let us love one another. . . .

—I Jn. 4:7

Reflection

1. What kind of endings do I like in stories? Why?
2. When I think of Easter, what kind of feelings do I get? What influence does Easter have on my personal life?
3. What makes Christ's resurrection appearance in Galilee especially moving?
4. Of what other stories does the lake-side appearance remind me?
5. What details from the resurrection narratives would my faith cite to testify to the reality of Christ's appearances?
6. If Jesus tested me publicly about my love for him, as he did Peter, how would I respond? What would I feel?
7. Jesus commissioned Peter to a leadership of love. How do I practice love leadership in my life?
8. Jesus also commissioned Peter to an institutional leadership as chief Shepherd. What is my response to this kind of leadership?
9. Jesus loved John as a personal friend. Why should I build personal friendships with those near me? What about loving everybody?
10. Why is it important that I practice making friends?

Prayer

Risen Jesus, you commissioned Peter to a leadership of love. You left me an example of a deep personal friendship with John. Grant that I may be a loving leader in my own area of authority. Help me to make friends among those near me that I may be open to love those in the wider world. Breathe your Spirit of love into my heart.